The Authorities

Powerful Wisdom from Leaders in the Field

ASTRID SCHMITT-BYLANDT

Entrepreneur, Mentor, Solution Finder

"Today felt like a huge step forward. I now realize there is nothing to fear. Thank you again you are amazing."
- Lloyd

"Thank you, Astrid you have been such a tremendous support, without you I would not have moved forward!"
- Shukri

"I do not know anybody else in my environment who so accurately analyzes any kind of interpersonal facts, distils the essence out of them and offers a working solution within a very short time. I thank Astrid from the bottom of my heart."
- Armin

Limits of Liability and Disclaimer of Warranty
The author and publisher shall not be liable for your misuse of the enclosed material. This book is strictly for informational and educational purposes.

Warning – Disclaimer
The purpose of this book is to educate and entertain. The author and/or publisher do not guarantee that anyone following these techniques, suggestions, tips, ideas, or strategies will become successful. The author and/or publisher shall have neither liability nor responsibility to anyone with respect to any loss or damage caused, or alleged to be caused, directly or indirectly by the information contained in this book.

Medical Disclaimer
The medical or health information in this book is provided as an information resource only, and is not to be used or relied on for any diagnostic or treatment purposes. This information is not intended to be patient education, does not create any patient-physician relationship, and should not be used as a substitute for professional diagnosis and treatment.

Publisher
Authorities Press
Markham, ON
Canada

Printed in the United States, Canada, and the United Kingdom.

FOREWORD

Experts are to be admired for their knowledge, but they often remain unrecognized by the general public because they save their information and insights for paying customers and clients. There are many experts in a given field, but their impact is limited to the handful of people with whom they work.

Unlike experts, authorities share their knowledge and expertise far more broadly, so they make a big impact on the world. Authorities become known and admired as leading experts and, as such, typically do very well economically and professionally. Most authorities are also mature enough to know that part of the joy of monetary success is the accompanying moral and spiritual obligation to give back.

Many people want to learn and work with well-respected and generous authorities, but don't always know where to find them. They may be known to their peers, or within a specific community, but have not had the opportunity to reach a wider audience. At one time, they might have submitted a proposal to the For Dummies or Chicken Soup for the Soul series of books, but it's now almost impossible to get accepted as a new author in such branded book series.

It is more than fitting that Raymond Aaron, an internationally known and respected authority in his own right, would be the one to recognize the need for a new venue in which authorities could share their considerable knowledge with readers everywhere. As the only author ever to be included in both of the book series mentioned above, Raymond has had the opportunity to give back and he understands how crucial it is for authorities to have a platform from which to share their expertise.

I have known and worked with Raymond for a number of years and consider him a valued friend and talented coach. He knows how to spot talented and knowledgeable people and he desires to see them prosper. Over the years, success coaching and speaking engagements around the world have made it possible for Raymond to meet many of these talented authorities. He recognizes and relates to their passion and enthusiasm for what they do, as well as their desire to share what they know. He tells me that's why he created this new nonfiction branded book series, *The Authorities*.

Dr. Nido Qubein
President, High Point University

TABLE OF CONTENTS

To my parents, especially my mum. Both have supported me throughout my life in their own ways, even though some ideas and projects of mine caused eyebrows to rise and heads to shake. Nevertheless, in the end, you supported me. Thank you!

To my true friends, who have been with me through thick and thin! Who supported me through moving to foreign countries, when I lost my job and when I opened my first business and the businesses afterwards. They were there when the businesses grew, through the ongoing ups and downs, and finally for my biggest wish to become a mum, which finally came true in early 2017 through IVF.

Thank you all for your support, for all your help, and for believing in me. I feel truly amazed, blessed, and am very, very grateful!

ACKNOWLEDGEMENTS

I would like to thank **Raymond Aaron** and his team for the many hours of support throughout my writing and their editing of my chapter. Also a big thank you to my lawyer, **Trevor Sears**, who I am incredibly grateful to, as he has been, and still is, a rock in the middle of a sometimes calm and sometimes rough business and life "ocean." He has had my back always. He has put me straight where I wandered off course and his character, which I once described as a mixture of Robin Hood and the Terminator, has been, and still is, a tremendous pillar in my life.

Equally, his former colleagues, **Paul Toolan** and **Philip Somarakis**, have and continue to be my support in hours of need and I am again truly grateful for all their help and advice.

I am grateful to my close friends, **Lutz Johnen, Dr. Alexander Zeisler, Egbert Hoppe, Charles Hudson, Michael Wood-Martin, Axel H. Günther, Ines Grund, Armin Klaus, Dr. Ulrich Hoppe, Dr. Monika Metzger, Dr. Rachael Abiss, Ben de Rivas, Peter Zanatta, Patrick Feuz, Arnd Brueggemann, Toni Muranyi, Dale Langan** (who was there with me when my children were born) and many more for taking the time to listen, help, support, and give the occasional reality check where I needed it. I feel truly blessed with all of you in my life!

Thank you to my past and current colleagues and suppliers who have become my friends who worked hard with me to help build and grow my businesses.

Thank you for my past, my present, and my future!

INTRODUCTION

Welcome to *The Authorities*. This is an anthology of ideas from individuals who have distinguished themselves in life and in business. They are authors who leave big footprints on the world, and as leaders in their particular fields, understand the importance and obligation of giving something back.

Authorities are not just experts. They are also known to be outstanding in their fields and in their communities. Because of this important difference, authorities are able to contribute more to humanity through both their chosen work and by giving back.

You will definitely know some of *The Authorities* in this book, especially since there are some world-famous ones. Others are just as exceptional, but you may not yet know about them. Our featured author, for example, is Astrid Schmitt-Bylandt.

When it comes to the challenges that you face in your life, the excuses for why you can't create change often fly fast. You simply move on, accepting that you can't do something without even challenging your reasons why.

In *Think in Solutions – Your Way to Success*, Astrid Schmitt-Bylandt shares the keys to her professional success and the growth of her businesses. She challenges you to stop accepting the excuse of "I can't". By giving you the keys necessary to think in solutions, Astrid also gives you the ability to get beyond that "I can't" excuse and create real change in all areas of your life.

As she shares these keys, Astrid also takes real life examples and uses them to illustrate how you may be sabotaging yourself, both personally and professionally. One of the main areas that Astrid focuses on is the excuses you might be telling yourself and the habits you have created to reinforce those different excuses.

Each aspect of this chapter involves asking yourself questions to change your thinking and shift your perception. It is not always easy to undo years of thinking and habits that have kept you from achieving success in different areas of your life. The goal of Astrid's *Think in Solutions* is to get you moving in the right direction by taking responsibility and acknowledging the power that you have, to create and build the life you want.

Recognize that this shift to thinking in solutions is going to mean that you must stop making assumptions about what is possible and start thinking outside of your status quo. That may include being open to changing your surroundings, the circle of people you move in and the way you deal with planning your days or dealing with any issue in your personal or business life. The process can be challenging, but once you shift your thinking, then you will never want to go back to the land of excuses. Start to *Think in Solutions* and find your way to success!

Enjoy this Authorities book, study it and take some of these great individuals up on their offers to do business with you. It might just be the best decision you ever make.

Think in Solutions – Your Way to Success

ASTRID SCHMITT-BYLANDT

How easy is it to say "this is not possible", or "I can't do this", or even worse, "you can't do this"? Then we move on and don't give the issues a second thought. I have these situations in my office every day and every time I challenge my colleagues by asking, "Imagine I wasn't here – what would you do?" Miraculously, everyone can always come up with a solution.

Don't get me wrong. That solution might not always be the one that we go with or one that works, but unless you change your thought process and your mindset, there will be many things that you are able to achieve but don't, because you are not even trying! When you feel like saying "I don't know how" or "that's not possible", make a point to always come up with at least ONE solution. Start today.

Different ways of changing thought processes work for different people. Make a list, write down all solutions you can come up with, even the funny, the weird and the "impossible" ones. Even the silly ones. Discuss the issue with someone you don't know that well to get a different perspective.

One of my friends challenged me the other day and asked me, "How about we do some magic and conjure up a perfect partner, boss or staff?" Yes, I know, magic has not exactly been perfected yet. However, by brainstorming and writing down all your thoughts, you can develop your list and start working towards your solutions. Once you start this habit you will come up with a variety of suggestions that you might not have initially thought about. Step by step, you will develop new thought processes.

So many people come up with the things that are "not possible" as it is so easy to focus on the negative. Make TODAY the day you stop this habit! Let today be the start of Thinking in Solutions!

In my office, I have five key points that everyone has to learn for growth and success:

1. Assumption is the mother of all f**k-ups.

2. Take responsibility for all your actions.

3. Be persistent – always chase and follow up.

4. Always connect with new people and continue building your network.

5. Think in Solutions!

The first four could fill a whole book but I will only go through them briefly in this chapter. However, the last point is a real passion of mine. People that have taken my training and/or in my employment that understand this, progress is exponential. It is phenomenal to watch their improvement and development every single time. (For more in-depth details, please visit my website at www.solutions-finder.com, see how I can help you find your solution.)

Last year, one of my colleagues told me that a specific castle and garden in England was not allowing groups for sightseeing. I asked for the phone number and spoke to the person in charge. Let's call him Jim. We chatted for a few minutes and then I told Jim about our client who really wanted to see the castle and gardens. I told Jim that our client was coming from abroad and would there be any way this group's visit could be made possible within the set of restrictions of the castle.

I simply asked if this could be made possible. I worked around HIS and his company's needs, and I tried to find common ground. He said ok but only in the afternoons and the group could not have their own guide. They would need to go through as individuals. That was ok with the group and EVERYONE was happy. I offered to pre-pay for the entrance fees immediately and when it came to booking again this year, Jim was happy to take another two groups the same way. Despite initially being told it was not possible, I was able to work out a deal that worked for everyone.

Think: What can I do for you? What would work for you? How can I help you?

A few years ago, I helped one of my friends who produces high quality rain and greywater harvesting solutions for airports, housing and other big building projects, to get an appointment with a specific engineer, who seemed to be blocking my friend's systems for all of his construction projects. My friend found it impossible to get hold of this particular engineer. Again, I asked for the phone number, I picked up the phone, asked for the engineer, got him on the phone, and arranged a time for a meeting with my friend. Now you might think, everyone can get lucky. Of course! However, this barrier my friend had in his head regarding the engineer being hard to get hold of didn't exist for me. I picked up the phone as if to call my mum or my friends. In my mind, there was no issue. I had no negative thoughts on this. In fact, I had no thoughts other than wanting to schedule a meeting. Had the engineer not been in the office, I would have asked his colleague for a time to call back. If the engineer had still not picked up, I would have asked to have a meeting or phone conversation scheduled. If you really want something, then persistence is one way to bring solutions.

Think: Be results driven and never give up!

For me, the word 'no' from someone else just doesn't resonate unless I have tried myself. Of course, it's not always possible to get someone to say 'yes'. You might say, "I can't go over my boss's head" or "I can't constantly do other people's work if they don't achieve what they should". No, I am not saying you should. You also have to cut your losses and think about what your time is worth to YOU. Perhaps your time is spent better achieving something else. Are there other ways or other things that you should be doing instead? Just because I can spend a lot of time on achieving something that others tell me is not possible doesn't mean I should necessarily do it.

However, it is crucial that, in order to start thinking in solutions, you change your thought process. Ask yourself if anyone famous you can think of could achieve what you want to achieve and might get a 'yes' in a situation that you feel is 'impossible'. If the answer is "yes," then your focus needs to be:

- How do you think they would do it?

4

- How can I or we make it possible?

- What does it need?

- Who could I ask for help?

- What solutions can I or we think of?

Money, I hear you say, is what makes most things happen. And yes, you are right. If you have a lot of money, you can employ more people. It's easier to ask people for favors and you might have a bigger network of people with skills, talents and contacts. Yes, money makes it easier, but that doesn't mean that things are otherwise impossible!

Solutions come in a variety of forms. Brainstorming is just one way. Always keep in mind: different people equal different views. Talk to your work team as well as the few key people that are part of your inner circle. Speak to the people from your sports groups or any of the groups that you might belong to. Ignore your habit of thinking that the issue might be difficult or impossible. Start fresh, every time! If your mind is focused on solutions, creating new ways and thinking about new routes and methods will become second nature. You'll surprise yourself with what you can actually achieve in life, in love and in work.

Think: If you need new inspiration, change your surroundings.

Change the people that you speak to about your issues. Change the environment you are sitting in or working in, or even where and how you sit. Change your lunch or dinner routines. Change your route to work or your gym routine. Give yourself a chance to gain different perspectives. Start meeting new people. Start networking with different people from different professional and social circles. Start new evening courses, read new books, find new things to do in your spare time. Nothing should keep you from finding the solutions that will lead you towards your path of success.

START WITH YOUR ROUTINES AND YOUR LANGUAGE

Often, we don't even notice when something has become a routine or a habit. Our minds do it on autopilot. We may get to our destination without having a conscious memory of the events that got us there. Even when there's a shift in our routine, it can be hard to break habits and we might find ourselves continuing to follow the same path because it's convenient or easier.

A few weeks ago, my normal route to work was blocked. I had to take a detour. Even on day two, three and four, I forgot that my "normal" route was closed. For days, I drove around the corner of my house right into the "road ahead closed" sign. I am sure we have all been in that situation before. We do something every day and it becomes a this-is-how-it's-meant-to-be way.

Actively find other ways and always know that you have the power to act.

Your daily routines often dictate your reality. Stop for a moment and think about what you did yesterday. Make one small change TODAY.

I can already hear the excuses about why it is not possible to change your life:

- But I can't...

- But how?

- But my kids, husband, family, boss, friends, etc.

- But I don't know...

- But I don't have the money…

- But I don't have time…

STOP!

Start with the mindset of searching for your solutions. Finish with the mindset that is focused on the obstacles. Time and money are something we can all make if it is important enough!

Think: Stop your routines – replace them with new ways.

DAILY LIFE SCENARIOS THAT CRY OUT FOR NEW SOLUTIONS

These are a few typical scenarios I see in my coaching sessions. Within a short chapter I can, of course, only scratch the surface of how things can be worked on and tackled. But here are a few examples:

Relationships

If your relationship is on the brink of failure, start by asking yourself:

1. What does my partner want from this relationship? (yes, start with your partner and not with yourself!)

2. What do I want from this relationship?

3. How can we successfully move forward setting goals and breaking them down into small steps?

4. What is the measurement to know when I have achieved step one?

5.   What can I do to take the next step?

Then set steps two, three and four - one at a time.

Implement each small step immediately and start the change now! Remember, though, it might well be that what the other side wants is just not what you want. Sometimes, it is time to move on. However, without starting to find common solutions, you will continue in the same rut, day in, day out.

Moving house

You want a new house? Then go out and find it! Define what it is that you want, where you want to live, how you want to live - SEE where and how you want to live! Visualize! Paint a picture or cut out the kind of housing that you can see yourself living in from ads or magazines. Go to the areas you want to live in, check the schools, the bars, the sports clubs or whatever it is you are looking for. Analyze your situation and determine what your options are. Do you have enough money for a deposit? Can you re-mortgage your current home? Can you sell your home and then move? Can you borrow money? Can you make extra money by taking in a lodger for a period of time to build up your savings? Can you move to a different area which is cheaper or closer to work or your children's school? Can you save money by doing or not doing things? Can you rent out a room to a language school and take in a student for a few months each year? Can you rent out a room on Airbnb? Tackle the "what" and "where" first and then tackle the financial side exactly the same way. But again, you need to start and take action NOW.

I won't go into the financial side as many books have been published about this and one paragraph will not do it justice. However, I would like to mention this sudden realization from one of my staff. I'll call her Rita:

Rita: "I just bought my lunch. I bought one of the plastic bags to carry the stuff back to the office. The bag costs GBP 0.10, which is not that much. But, if I went shopping three times a week and had started shopping at 10 years old, by the time I turned 90 I would have spent GBP1,248 in plastic shopping bags!!! That's two holidays for me!!"

New job needed

Unhappy with your job? Then find a new one! Easier said than done, some of you will say. Whatever the reasons you might have for not changing there is a solution! Focus on the positive even if you have been unemployed! What skills do you have? What makes you happy all day, every day? What do you really want to work in? What new qualifications might you need? How can you get them? Who can you ask to help you prepare your CV or prepare you for interviews? Who can you ask who might know someone in the field you would like to go into? What do you love doing? Who does what you do or want to do? Find that person who is successful at what you would like to do! See if you can work with or for them. If necessary, offer to work for free for a week or more to show that you are the right person for the job. If that is not possible, try and work on a few weekends or in the evenings. Find five or ten potential ways and explore all of them to find your perfect solution. Adjust your outcomes each time to move in the right direction.

Decide:

1.   What is it that I actually want?

2.   What and how does that look like and feel like?

3.   What do I believe is holding me back?

4.   How can I solve the issues that I believe are holding me back?

5.   What is the timeframe I want this change to happen in?

6.   Who can I ask for help?

Start researching your new job options. Start scheduling those interviews. Plan for what you are looking for. Are you a part-time mum interested in a part-time job? Or, do you want a bit more income as a pensioner or perhaps the multi-million-pound new job! Focus on what you want and work on finding the right solution every day.

Every new step has to be planned and you have to start TODAY! Just like learning how to walk, take a baby step each day. Only you can take these steps. No one will do it for you.

Actively change your ways. Get those different perspectives. Shake up your routine by trying something new or different. You can't reap the benefits of change without shifting your mindset and perceptions. You have to find the right solutions for yourself.

Think: Action, even in the form of a small step, is a step in the right direction!

THE ADVANTAGE OF COACHING

Remember when your parents, siblings or teachers said, "Do you want to learn how to walk, talk? Play the piano? Play tennis, football, etc.?" Each day you improved a little bit by following a step by step process. Today, you can swim, play tennis, speak a language, or whatever you started learning in your earlier years.

If, today, you had someone who said, "I know how to do what you want to achieve. I'll take you by the hand and walk with you, come what may," wouldn't you immediately say, "YES. Please show me!"

FIND that person who has done what you want to do.

FIND that person who will listen to what you want to achieve, who can teach you what you would like to learn and hold you responsible when you slack. Be proactive and persistent in looking for the solutions that are right for YOU.

Think and write down: What do I want to achieve and what are all the ways I can think of to start me on my journey to success?

Unfortunately, as children, we don't always appreciate free education. However, as an adult, education can be expensive. All too often, we wish we had learnt languages, math, etc. at school, studied harder or been taught X-Y-Z subject, for example, business, media, making/managing money, setting up your own business, etc. There is no back to the future time machine yet but you can move forward! It is never too late to start afresh with anything you would like to have and enjoy!

My mum found love after my dad died when she was 74. She turned 92 this August and what an amazing 18 years they have already shared and hopefully, they will have many more years to come of travelling, going out and appreciating each other's company. Remember, it is never too late!

If you are ready to learn, then you can find online courses, free YouTube tutorials, sports classes, evening classes and, of course, mentors and coaches. I have helped many people through their life's crises over the years. It took a long time to fully realize that this is a skill that I hugely enjoy. I have supported many people move forward in life and achieve their goals. Now I finally made this into my perfect job. I started looking at patterns in what I was doing, and

I started thinking about how to use this to help not just my friends and my family. Since the beginning of the year I started training unemployed people to be able to go back to work. It is one of the most rewarding things I have done in my life (only beaten by having children on my own through IVF – but that's a different story).

Everyone can find a course or a trainer, a mentor or a coach. See if they have achieved what you want to achieve and work with them to set your targets and your steps. Hopefully, they can hold you accountable every step of the way and help you remain focused and disciplined, which will, therefore, achieve your desired outcome and successes.

No matter what it is that you want, there is a solution! It might require you to think outside the box, but once you do, then the possibilities are endless. How do you get the type of mindset that will have you focused on solutions?

It starts by retraining your brain to look for the positive. See challenges and address them, instead of seeing obstacles that are blocking your path to success. Accept that it can be difficult to shift your mindset after years of experiences that shaped your way of looking at your world. Give yourself some credit for starting small and being persistent! (And if you have children start them as early as possible on their "yes I can do this" way through life!)

Now, you might not realize this but language also plays a huge part in your daily achievements and your thought processes. You might not immediately think about how words and language can have a massive influence, so I would like to set a challenge for you:

For seven days, stop for a few seconds every time you THINK or SAY something negative!

If you want to keep track, open a document on your mobile phone and write down how many times a day you say something negative about work, friends, your colleagues or about your health, partner, family members or whatever you think or talk about. You'll be amazed, if you are honest with yourself, by just how many times every day you think negatively and don't even realize it. Both mentally and verbally we need to make ourselves aware every hour of the day how we think and what consequences this has on our behavior, perception and actions.

Here's a challenge for the second week: stop yourself before you say something negative and consider putting it into a positive phrase.

Instead of shouting for the tenth time at your child for not having done something you asked, take a deep breath and explain the issue. Rather than scolding or punishment, which so far has never really given you the result you have wanted, find a solution to move forward.

Instead of slagging off your colleague, just say nothing or try and actually compliment him or her. Find that one positive thing that you see in him or her.

If you know that your partner "always" forgets something, is always late, or whatever he or she might do, anticipate it. Offer your help if you are better at it and find a solution together so you can both relax.

Changing both your thought processes and your language is key to any change.

Of course, some things are harder to get done on your own. That's why working with someone who can shake up your routines, who can remind you of your goals and achievements and who can re-focus you, can be a huge source of motivation. I love my job. I love helping people who are feeling stuck in a difficult situation in their lives, shifting their mindset and helping them to set and achieve their goals. Find that person that can be your 'go to Person' to move forward.

REALIZE THE IMPACT OF YOUR HABITS, PRIORITIES AND BELIEFS

One of the realities of creating any change in your life involves recognizing how your routines, and also your habits, impact your life. That can often be harder than you realize, but once you start the process of being honest with yourself and shifting your thinking, then the impact of your habits, your priorities and your beliefs will become apparent.

One of my clients who is unemployed talked about his goal of writing his own book and opening his own small business. Throughout the process, he has taken in so much and has already moved miles forward. I am thrilled with his progress, but when we started talking about making healthy food choices, the excuses started to fly.

"I'm not good at that, it costs so much" or "What is healthy anyway?"

Every response was an excuse about why changing his eating habits was not possible. So, to help him shift his thinking, I started with something that I knew he could do, regardless of budget or time.

"Well, you can start with drinking eight free glasses of tap water every day," I said.

"Eight?"

He looked at me for a minute as if I had asked him to do something extraordinary. I confirmed that I had said eight. "Ah, I can't do this," he said.

"Why? It is free and it is so simple."

Then I shifted the topic to his dog. His eyes lit up and he spoke with such love and gratitude for his dog. "He is the one keeping me sane through my dark times, but he is old now and has hip problems," he said.

"Do you walk him every day?" I asked.

"Of course!"

"Do you feed him every day?"

"Of course!"

"And when he is thirsty, do you give him water?"

"Of course!"

"So, you look after your dog, but not yourself?"

After a long silence, he said, "Oh, I see."

Sometimes, we know what we need to do, but we don't really realize it. Or rather, we know what to do, but we choose not to act. Take the issues in your life and imagine that someone else told you about those same problems in their life. What would you say to them? What solutions would you present to them?

Write down the options that you would suggest to someone else. Then write down all your thoughts regarding the situation. Include a list of all the objections that you might have. For each objection, I challenge you to come up with one positive answer. You need to be actively searching for solutions. It is about training yourself to think in a new way, one that allows you to tap into your creative mind and the solutions that are locked up inside your mind.

The reality is that you most likely have the answers, but you are blocking them with whatever excuse you have been telling yourself. I want you to change your habits to break through those blockades. But right now, that might feel a bit overwhelming.

So, by taking small steps, you can take action daily to implement just one of the positive solutions you found. Work on them until that solution becomes one of your new habits. You will know it has truly become a habit when you don't think about it anymore, just like when you are driving a car. Then move on to the next point.

Changing a habit starts with:

- defining your goal
- finding out what your false beliefs are that hinder you and hold you back
- breaking your goal down into smaller steps
- creating a timeframe for achieving each of those smaller steps
- finding motivation by defining the "WHY"
- moving forward by completing the smaller steps

It is possible to stop habits from one day to the other, like it is possible to stop smoking, but it needs a lot more discipline and effort than many of us are willing to invest. So set for yourself small steps and small goals!

You need to actively replace every small step you set for yourself and stay focused on the solutions you have set out and defined for yourself. Each habit you replace will allow you to then shift to another one. Creating any change in your life, small or major, begins with these small changes.

Always seek positive reinforcement as that is the key to inspiring continued action. If you are trying to change everything at once, the process becomes overwhelming, and our tendency is to just give up. I want you to manage the process of change. I want the process and the small successes to motivate you and keep you moving forward.

BE CREATIVE – LOOK FOR OPPORTUNITIES EVEN WHERE YOU WOULDN'T EXPECT THEM

This tool is priceless, from working with your children or your family to working in your job, with your team, or on your relationship.

Last week, I had to take my car to a car wash. I had to do it with my 2-year-old twins, which most parents will agree is not as easy as when you do it on your own. I had to keep my children occupied for 30 minutes so we went for a walk. Now, not many 2-year-olds are hugely keen on going for a walk. They don't see that exercise is good for everyone.

As we walked through the streets, I found an empty beer can and for the next 30 minutes, we kicked the beer can through the streets back towards the garage where the shiny clean car was waiting for us. Time had flown by, even for me, and neither the picture of an empty beer can in the street nor the vision of a walk for 30 minutes while waiting for the car to be cleaned would have thrilled anyone. This walk was different! An empty beer can made it fun.

I know, you can't kick a beer can around the office, you can't kick it around at home – but you CAN take nearly any task and break it down in chunky sizes and there will always be some kind of positive angle to it. Even if it only means you got it done and can cross it off your to do list! Feel the feeling of achievement!

Think: What will make my work easier or even fun?

Are there areas in your life where you might be missing out because you are stuck seeing your world from a perspective that no longer serves you? I want you to stop looking at a situation from the same point of view and find other ways of tackling and thinking about this issue or situation. If you have discussed it with other people, and you are not getting any further, be creative! Imagine you were a famous person. How would he or she go about it? Or if you are less into this kind of creative thinking and more logical, then be creative on paper. Write a SWOT analysis (strengths, weaknesses, opportunities, threats) or just put a pros and cons list together.

START TODAY and your reality will start to shift! You will truly amaze yourself at the possibilities and opportunities that will come your way!

Even if your circumstances do not change right away, changing how you view those circumstances will allow for a change in attitude, which will lead to change in your life.

Every point in this chapter has focused on you finding solutions by opening your mind and shifting your perception. Now I want to question whether you are actually being honest with yourself and taking responsibility for your life choices or if you are essentially hiding with your head in the sand.

TAKING RESPONSIBILITY STARTS WITH HONESTY

How good are you at taking responsibility for your own actions? Be honest with yourself!

Today's culture focuses on blaming others and using circumstances outside of our control as the reason why we react or behave a certain way. It's easier to feel like a victim than to take responsibility for our own actions.

Not long after I had joined a new company, which required me to move from Germany to London, my former boss told me that it was my fault that one of the hotel contractors had missed the assigned deadline. That contractor had received the deadline from me two months earlier. Her inactions meant we lost a huge piece of business. I was livid! I had gone out and gained the client's trust, asking my boss that the company spend money on a sales trip. I had done my sales job, and now I got the blame for losing the business?! The contractor hadn't even looked at the file for the whole past two months. I was at fault? Not her?

It was a learning experience for me, one that I took with me, eventually to open my own first business. First, though, I immediately changed my way of working. Every request was put into a separate file. I started keeping count of the work that I had passed to the contributing departments. I started to chase everything! I was determined that this was never going to happen to me again.

Think: Always take responsibility!

Today as a business owner, I can better understand my former boss's point of view. It was a big piece of business, one that needed to be managed and monitored throughout the process and that should have been my job and, of course, it was in my interest to check for updates. However, I also learnt that if a member of staff can be allowed to sit on a piece of business with no one checking on the progress, then process and management also need to be checked and changed. The internal systems of each business, of course, also need to be thoroughly reviewed and analyzed.

Today, therefore, the first person I always hold accountable is myself. The responsibility for the success or failure of my businesses always lies first and foremost with me. When you are trying to make a significant change in your life or career, it can be difficult to be honest with yourself and acknowledge how you may have contributed to an outcome you didn't desire. Without that acknowledgment and honesty, however, you cannot learn and grow from your experiences.

You might not always like what you find, but if you are not honest with yourself, then you can't make changes, create a different outcome or move forward.

Think: What can I do to move things forward and what is my responsibility?

If you truly want change in your life, analyze each section and ask yourself honestly what your current status quo is.

What are you willing to accept from yourself? Where do you want to go and WHO do you want to be or become? Whether it be in family life, as a parent, as a boss, as a colleague, in your sports achievement or as a partner. Create your vision!

Push yourself out of your comfort zone! Yes, it might sometimes be uncomfortable!

It definitely was uncomfortable to hear what my boss had to say, but it allowed me to rethink my way of working, my way of thinking and to do what was necessary to change and improve the situation, both then and in my future. Mistakes are there to be made but make them just once!

Here are a few questions to help you start shifting your thinking into solution-based thinking and help you identify the ways that you might be falling into the "blame game":

• What do or did I contribute to my current circumstances, both personally and professionally?

• Have I been open to taking risks and stepping outside of my comfort zone?

- Where am I blaming others, or circumstances, rather than taking responsibility to move forward?

- Are the things that are holding me back in the past and therefore cannot be changed?

- How can I accept the past and learn to move forward?

- What small step can I set today to move me on the road for change and success?

Are you willing to break out of your comfort zone? Are you willing to really be honest with yourself? Only you are in charge of your life and it is important to take responsibility for it!

WHAT IS THE BLAME GAME?

I want to stop for a minute and talk about the blame game. Simply put, it is when you are dealing with various situations in your life and choose to blame others for your situation. You believe you are the victim, instead of focusing on what you could do to change the situation NOW. You are essentially giving away your power and allowing others to control your life. The thought process turns into one that makes everything appear impossible and out of your control, so you sit, stuck, doing nothing at all to create change in your life.

I see some of this in my clients that are unemployed. The system especially twenty or more years ago wasn't set up to identify ADHD or dyslexia or other forms of learning disabilities. Parents might have not been able to help financially or mentally and once someone is at the bottom it really is hard to get up again. Not to mention, many companies do not even give people a chance to prove themselves.

However, this absolutely does not mean you should give up! The past is the past and can never be changed. Now is the time to take responsibility, move forward, make changes, listen, learn, forgive and make that leap! Be responsible, be on time, be reliable and be flexible! All these actions anyone can do, regardless of your situation.

Here are some questions to ask yourself as you deal with various situations in your life:

- Do you blame someone for something in your life?

- Do you blame a situation for something that went wrong in your life?

- Do you appear to take responsibility, but then turn around and immediately start focusing on the actions of others?

- Do you compare your choices and actions with others, judging them as better or worse?

- Are you letting others rule your life?

- Are you not taking action because you believe nothing can be done?

Think: Let the past lie, accept what cannot be changed and take action to have that better future you deserve!

CREATING ACTIONS

No matter what circumstances we all are presented with in life, we still have the ability to act. You still control your thoughts and feelings. No one else has that control, nor should they! Even in old age you can take action, so age is no excuse! Do not become so focused on finding excuses that you block yourself from opening doors and creating opportunities for yourself.

A few weeks ago, as I sat to have a relaxing manicure, the TV screen on the wall showed a Ninja UK program where amazing young men and women go over very intense courses, challenging their own fitness, agility and power. One candidate even had only one leg.

A very big lady sitting next to me said, "Oh, I want him to win. How amazing is he!"

When coming across one exercise, which was already hugely difficult for the candidates with two legs, he failed and fell into the pool below.

The lady turned around to her waiting husband and said, "Wow, that makes me want to go to the gym."

Not in a million years did I think that she would go home and start working out. You WISH you were as fit, but you are unwilling to put in the hard work. Instead, we spend our energy coming up with excuses for why things can't get done. The reality is that you are making up reasons why you won't do it.

Think: What excuses are you using to justify why you aren't taking action?

There are so many excuses that we create to justify why we refuse to act and create change in our lives. Why do we wish for things but then take no action?

- Because it seems too hard.
- Because it seems too tiring.
- Because there does not seem to be enough time.

- Because, because, because.....

The list is long. However, there is so much that is possible when you only open up your mind and heart!

Think: The possibilities in my life are endless if I only embrace them!

Inaction, a lack of honesty with yourself and not taking responsibility are just a few of the key reasons why you might be struggling to create change in your life. By acknowledging how these reasons contribute to your current situation, you begin to change. Once you decide to change your thinking and perception, then you need to find others who support you in these efforts.

NETWORKING: BUILDING SUPPORT FOR CHANGE

One of the things so many people are afraid of seems to be networking. What is it about going to an event and talking to strangers that people worry about? Everyone is there for the same reasons. What is the worst that can happen?

You can expand your network and increase the resources available to you professionally and personally. New networks are also great ways to find individuals who can help hold you accountable or even offer you different choices for work or life. Also remember, these people also know others who might be able to help with your challenges and efforts or, of course, you can help them!

I constantly encourage people to look at who they are surrounding themselves with. Be honest with yourself about the type of thinking they represent.

Think: Is it the type of thinking you want to make a part of your life? Do THEY lead the life you want for yourself?

Leave "friends" behind that shoot people down. They are no friends if they don't support you. They only keep you around to make themselves feel better by belittling you. Move on, there are new people to be met who will believe in what you want to achieve, and who live and breathe the solutions you need.

The people you surround yourself with can also serve as inspiration. They can get you motivated to keep tackling various challenges in your life, instead of giving up. Feelings of frustration can become blockades in your efforts to be solution oriented in your thinking.

Our inner circle, those people who support us, can be the way that you break through frustration, barriers and problems. They might even provide a few solutions you never thought of.

The more you surround yourself with solution-focused individuals, the more you will think in solutions. The same is true when you are trying to change habits or create new ones. Let's talk about how to shift them without being overwhelmed in the process.

Building a network involves finding places with like-minded individuals, be it personally or professionally. If you are looking to build a professional network, then start with industry events where you can meet other professionals who can point you to various opportunities.

Personal networking often starts with self-empowerment and growth opportunities. It could be mastermind classes or attending talks specifically focused on areas that you are trying to grow in. The point of any class or talk is about not only learning, but meeting others. You make connections that help you grow, but you might also prove to be a connection that allows them to grow.

Why should you build a network?

Here are a few of the key reasons:

- to help you explore new solutions to your challenges
- to help you meet others with different perspectives
- to challenge yourself to stretch your abilities
- for support in making shifts, personally or professionally
- to find the people to help you grow and become successful in what you want to do
- to give advice and support to others who may be in a situation similar to one you are or were in

Networking opportunities are available in a variety of areas. You can opt to search online for networking opportunities, such as those for local business owners. If you are looking for opportunities to create change in the community, then look for community get-togethers where you can meet others and build support. Or find a local charity, a new sport you can take up – the opportunities are endless.

The point is that finding networking opportunities often starts by just opening your mind and having the willingness to extend yourself beyond your current status quo. I always encourage people to build or extend their network, because doing so will give more opportunities to grow and learn. You might be thinking, "I don't have time to network. My schedule is already so full."

I understand what it means to be a busy professional. Being a single mother to my truly amazing twins and running my businesses, as well as all of my other professional endeavors, means that my schedule often seems to be running me. To make time for new networking opportunities every now and then, I have focused on prioritizing, systemizing, working hard and, where possible, delegating. It helps me to manage all my obligations and to make time for everything in my life that I find valuable, both personally and professionally. And if you still find it daunting to go networking, then come on our networking course or search for one in your area.

FINDING MOTIVATION IN YOUR LIFE

We all need motivation. I think of it as the key necessary to get the car started. Without it, you are not going anywhere. You don't start you go nowhere! However, once you start every small success will feed more success and in return will fuel your motivation.

The idea is to keep yourself motivated through the progress you make. Another way to remain motivated is of course through mentors or coaches.

Once I stared looking for and working with my mentors I truly got inspired and motivated to tackle the challenges in my life and find my solutions. Mentors keep you on your toes, and for me they continue to show me new ways of thinking that inspire me to learn and grow; every day!

Not only is it important to work with mentors, you also learn when you teach yourself. Mentoring others gives you a chance to reinforce, in your own mind, the ways that you want to think and act.

Taking action involves work, but once you get started, you will be amazed at how much better you feel. Your world will start to change because you have changed your way of thinking.

Do not be afraid to take the first steps to create change by shifting your thinking and perceptions. Once you make that shift, then you are going to find it easier to build a network, change your habits and start on the path of growth and finding solutions. My professional life benefited when I stopped making excuses or finding others to blame. The lessons I learned carried into my businesses and my personal life have assisted me in every goal that I have achieved so far.

No matter where you are in terms of your personal or professional life, do not assume that it is too late to take risks or that you cannot change. You have the power of YES to create the life that you want. It starts by changing your thinking, from searching for problems to being solution oriented.

Connect with Astrid and her team at www.solutions-finder.com and share your journey with them to find the solutions for your challenges. On the website you can share stories, learn about Astrid's events, and become the more successful YOU!

Step Into Greatness

LES BROWN

You have greatness within you. You can do more than you could ever imagine. The problem most people have is that they set a goal and then ask "how can I do it? I don't have the necessary skills or education or experience".

I know what that's like. I wasted 14 years on asking myself how I could be a motivational speaker. My mind focused on the negative—on the things that were in my way, rather than on the things that were not.

It's not what you don't have but what you think you need that keeps you from getting what you want from life. But, when the dream is big enough, the obstacles don't matter. You'll get there if you stay the course. Nothing can stop you but death itself.

Think about that last statement for a minute. There's nothing on this earth that can stop you from achieving what it is that you want. So, get out of your way, and quit sabotaging your dreams. Do everything in your power to make them happen—because you cannot fail!

They say the best way to die is with your loved ones gathered around your bed. But what if you were dying and it was the ideas you never acted upon, the gifts you never used and the dreams you never pursued, that were circled around your bed? Answer that question right now. Write down your answers. If you die this very moment what ideas, what gifts, what dreams will die with you?

Then say: I refuse to die an unlived life! You beat out 40 million sperm to get here, and you'll never have to face such odds again. Walk through the field of life and leave a trail behind.

One day, one of my rich friends brought my mother a new pair of shoes for me. Now, even though we weren't well off, I didn't want them; they were a size nine and I was a size nine and a half. My mother didn't listen and told my sister to go get some Vaseline, which she rubbed all over my feet. Then my mother had me put those shoes on, minding that I didn't scrunch down the heel. She had my sister run some water in the bathtub, and I was told to get in and walk around in the water. I said that my feet hurt. She just ignored me and asked about my day at school, how everything went and did I get into any fights? I knew what she was up to, that she was trying to distract me, so I said I had only gotten into three fights. After a while mother asked me if my feet still hurt. I admitted that the pain had indeed lessened. She kept me walking in that tub until I had a brand new pair of comfortable, size nine and a half shoes.

You see, once the leather in the shoes got wet, they stretched! And what you need to do is stretch a little. I believe that most people don't set high goals and miss them, but rather, they set lower goals and hit them and then they stay there, stuck on the side of the highway of life. When you're pursuing your greatness, you don't know what your limitations are, and you need to act like you don't have any. If you shoot for the moon and miss, you'll still be in the stars.

You also need coaching (a mentor). Why? There are times you, too, will find yourself parked on the side of the highway of life with no gas in the vehicle. What you need then is someone to stop and offer to pick up some gas down the road a ways and bring it back to you. That person is your coach. Yes, they are there for advice, but their main job is to help you through the difficulties that life throws at all of us.

Another reason for having a coach is that you can't see the picture when you're in the frame. In other words, he or she can often see where you are with a clarity and focus that's unavailable to you. They're not going to leave you parked along the road of life, nor are they going to allow you to be stuck in the moment like a photo in a frame.

And let's say you just can't see you're way forward. You don't believe it's possible. Sometimes you just have to believe in someone's belief in you. This could be your coach, a loved one or even a staunch friend. You need to hear them say you can do it, time and again. Because, after all, faith comes from hearing and hearing and hearing.

Look at it this way. Most people fail because of possibility blindness. They can't see what lies before them. There are always possibilities. Because of this, your dream is possible. You may fail often. In fact, I want you to say this: I will fail my way to success. Here is why.

I had a TV show that failed. I felt I had to go back to public speaking. I had failed, so I parked my car for ten years. Then I saw Dr. Wayne Dyer was still on PBS and I decided to call them. They said they would love to work with me and asked where I had been. I wasn't as good as I had been ten years before, as I was out of practice, but I still had to get back in the game. I was determined to drive on empty.

Listen to recordings, go to seminars, challenge yourself, and you'll begin to step into your greatness, you'll begin to fill yourself with the energy you need to climb to ever greater heights. Most people never attend a seminar. They won't invest money in books or audio programs. You put yourself in the top 5 percent just by making a different choice than the average person. This is called contrary thinking. It's a concept taken from the financial industry. One considers choosing the exact opposite behaviour of the average person as a way to get better than average results. You don't have to make the contrarian choice, but if you don't have anything to lose by going that road, why not consider the option?

Make your move before you're ready. Walk by faith not by sight and make sure you're happy doing it. If you can't be happy, what else is there? Helen Keller said, "Life is short, eat the dessert first."

What is faith? Many of us think of God when we think of faith. A different viewpoint claims that faith is a firm belief in something for which there is no proof. I would rather think of faith as something that is believed especially with strong conviction. It is this last definition I am referring to when I say walk by faith not by sight. Be happy and go forth with strong conviction that you are destined for greatness.

An important step on your way to greatness is to take the time to detoxify. You've got to look at the people in your life. What are they doing for you? Are they setting a pace that you can follow? If not, whose pace have you adjusted to? If you're the smartest in your group, find a new group.

Are the people in your life pulling you down or lifting you up? You know what to do, right? Banish the negative and stay with the positive; it's that simple. Dr. Norman Vincent Peale once said (when I was in the audience), "You are special. You have greatness within you, and you can do more than you could ever possibly imagine."

He overrode the inner conversations in my mind and reached the heart of me. He set me on fire. This is yet another reason for seeking out the help of a coach or mentor or other new people in your life. They can do what Dr. Peale did for me. They can set your passion free.

How important is it to have the right kind of person/people on your side? There was a study done that determined it takes 16 people saying you can do something to overcome one person who says you can't do something. That's right, one negative, unsupportive person can wipe out the work of 16 other supportive people. The message can't be any clearer than that.

Let's face the cold, hard truth: most people stay in park along the highway of life. They never feel the passion, the love for their fellow man, or for the work they do. They are stuck in the proverbial rut. What's the reason? There are many reasons, but only one common factor: fear — fear of change, fear of failure, fear of success, fear they may not be good enough, fear of competition, even fear of rejection.

"Rejection is a myth," says Jack Canfield, co-author of The Chicken Soup for the Soul series. "It's not like you get a slap in the face each time you are rejected." Why not take every "no" you receive as a vitamin, and every time you take one know you are another step closer to success.

You will win if you don't quit. Even a broken clock is right twice a day.

Professional baseball players, on average, get on base just three times out of every ten times they face the opposing pitcher. Even superstars fail half of the time they appear at the plate.

Top commissioned salespeople face similar odds. They may make one sale from every three people they see, but it will have taken them between 75 and 100 telephone calls to make the 15 appointments they need to close their five sales for the week. And these are statistics for the elite. Most salespeople never reach these kinds of numbers.

People don't spend their lives working for just one company anymore. This means you must build up a set of skills and experiences that are portable. This can be done a number of ways, but my favourite approaches follow.

You must be willing to do the things others won't do in order to have tomorrow the things that others don't have. Provide more service than you get paid for. Set some high standards for yourself.

Begin each day with your most difficult task. The rest of the day will seem more enjoyable and a whole lot easier.

Someone needs help with a problem? Be the solution to that problem.

Also, find those tasks that are being consistently ignored and do them. You'll be surprised by the results. An acquaintance of mine used this approach at a number of entry-level positions and each time he quickly ended up being offered a position in management.

You must increase your energy. Kick it up a notch. We are spirits having a physical existence; let your spirit shine. Quit frittering away your energy. Use it to move you closer to the achievement of your dreams. Refuse to spend it on non-productive activities.

What do people say about you when you leave a room? Are you willing to take responsibility—to walk your talk. There is a terrible epidemic sweeping our nation, and it is the refusal to take responsibility for one's actions. Consider that at some point in any situation there will have been a moment where you could have done something to change the outcome. To that end you are responsible for what happened. It's a hard thing to accept, but it's true.

Life's hard. It was hard when I was told I had cancer. I had sunken into despair, and was hiding away in my study when my son came in. My son asked me if I was going to die. What could I do? I told him I was going to fight, even though I was scared. I also told him that I needed some help. Not because I was weak but because I wanted to stay strong. Keep asking until you get help. Don't stop until you get it.

A setback is the setup for a comeback. A setback is simply a misstep on the long road of success. It means nothing in the larger scheme of things. And, surprisingly, it sets you up for your next win. It tends to focus you and your energy on your immediate goals, paving the way for your next sprint, for your comeback.

It's worth it. Your dreams are worth the sacrifices you'll have to make to achieve them. Find five reasons that will make your dreams worth it for you. Say to yourself, I refuse to live an unlived life.

If you are casual about your dreams, you'll end up a casualty. You must be passionate about your dreams, living and breathing them throughout your days. You've got to be hungry! People who are hungry refuse to take no for an answer. Make NO your vitamin. Be unstoppable. Be hungry.

Let me give you an example of what I mean by hungry ...

I decided I wanted to become a disc jockey, so I went down to the local radio station and asked the manager, Mr. Milton "Butterball" Smith, if he had a job available for a disc jockey. He said he did not. The next day I went back, and Mr. Smith asked "Weren't you here yesterday?" I explained that I was just checking to see if anyone was sick or had died. He responded by telling me not to come back again. Day three, I went back again—with the same story. Mr. Smith told me to get out of there. I came back the fourth day and gave Mr. Smith my story one more time. He was so beside himself that he told me to get him a cup of coffee. I said, "Yes, sir!" That's how I became the errand boy.

While working as an errand boy at the station, I took every opportunity to hang out with the deejays and to observe them working. After I had taught myself how to run the control room, it was just a matter of biding my time.

Then one day an opportunity presented itself. One of the disc jockeys by the name of Rockin' Roger was drinking heavily while he was on the air. It was a Saturday afternoon. And there I was, the only one there.

I watched him through the control-room window. I walked back and forth in front of that window like a cat watching a mouse, saying "Drink, Rock, Drink!" I was young. I was ready. And I was hungry.

Pretty soon, the phone rang. It was the station manager. He said, "Les, this is Mr. Klein."

I said, "Yes, I know."

He said, "Rock can't finish his program."

I said, "Yes sir, I know."

He said, "Would you call one of the other disc jockeys to fill in?"

I said, "Yes sir, I sure will, sir."

And when he hung up, I said, "Now he must think I'm crazy." I called up my mama and my girlfriend, Cassandra, and I told them, "Ya'll go out on the front porch and turn up the radio, I'M ABOUT TO COME ON THE AIR!"

I waited 15 or 20 minutes and called the station manager back. I said, "Mr. Klein, I can't find NOBODY!"

He said, "Young boy, do you know how to work the controls?"

I said, "Yes, sir."

He said, "Go in there, but don't say anything. Hear me?"

I said, "Yes, sir."

I couldn't wait to get old Rock out of the way. I went in there, took my seat behind that turntable, flipped on the microphone and let 'er rip.

"Look out, this is me, LB., triple P. Les Brown your platter-playin' papa. There were none before me and there will be none after me, therefore that makes me the one and only. Young and single and love to mingle, certified, bona fide and indubitably qualified to bring you satisfaction and a whole lot of action. Look out baby, I'm your LOVE man."

I WAS HUNGRY!

During my adult life I've been a deejay, a radio station manager, a Democrat in the Ohio Legislature, a minister, a TV personality, an author and a public speaker, but I've always looked after what I valued most—my mother. What I want for her is one of my dreams, one of my goals.

My life has been a true testament to the power of positive thinking and the infinite human potential. I was born in an abandoned building on a floor in Liberty City, a low-income section of Miami, Florida, and adopted at six weeks of age by Mrs. Mamie Brown, a 38-year-old single woman, cafeteria cook and domestic worker. She had very little education or financial means, but a very big heart and the desire to care for myself and my twin brother. I call myself Mrs. Mamie Brown's Baby Boy and I say that all that I am and all that I ever hoped to be, I owe to my mother.

My determination and persistence in searching for ways to help my mother overcome poverty and developing my philosophy to do whatever it takes to achieve success led me to become a distinguished authority on harnessing human potential and success. That philosophy is best expressed by the following ...

"If you want a thing bad enough to go out and fight for it,
to work day and night for it,
to give up your time, your peace and your sleep for it...
if all that you dream and scheme is about it,
and life seems useless and worthless without it...
if you gladly sweat for it and fret for it and plan for it
and lose all your terror of the opposition for it...
if you simply go after that thing you want
with all of your capacity, strength and sagacity,
faith, hope and confidence and stern pertinacity...
if neither cold, poverty, famine, nor gout,
sickness nor pain, of body and brain,
can keep you away from the thing that you want...
if dogged and grim you beseech and beset it,
with the help of God, you will get it!"

Branding
Small Business

RAYMOND AARON

Branding is an incredibly important tool for creating and building your business. Large companies have been benefiting from branding ever since people first started selling things to other people. Branding made those businesses big.

If you're a small business owner, you probably imagine that small companies are different and don't need branding as much as large companies do. Not true. The truth is small businesses need branding just as much, if not more, than large companies.

Perhaps you've thought about branding, but assumed you'd need millions of dollars to do it properly, or that branding is just the same thing as marketing. Nothing could be further from the truth.

Marketing is the engine of your company's success. Branding is the fuel in that engine.

In the old days, salespeople were a big part of the selling process. They recommended one product over another and laid out the reasons why it was better. Salespeople had credibility because they knew about all the products, and customers often took the advice they had to offer.

Today, consumers control the buying process. They shop in big box stores, super-sized supermarkets, and over the Internet — where there are no salespeople. Buyers now get online and gather information beforehand. They learn about all the products available and look to see if there really is any difference between them. Consumers also read reviews and check social media to see if both the company and the product are reputable. In other words, they want to know what the brand is all about.

The way of commerce used to be: "Nothing happens till something is sold." Today it's: "Nothing happens till something is branded!"

DEFINING A BRAND

A brand is a proper name that stands for something. It lives in the consumer's mind, has positive or negative characteristics, and invokes a feeling or an image. In short, it's a person's perception of a product or a company.

When all goes well, consumers associate the same characteristics with a brand that the company talks about in its advertising, public relations, marketing and sales materials. Of course, when a product doesn't live up to what the company says about it, the brand gets a bad reputation. On the other hand, if a product or service over-delivers on the promises made, the brand can become a superstar.

RECOGNIZING BRANDING AND ITS CHARACTERISTICS

Branding is the science and art of making something that isn't unique, unique. Branding in the marketplace is the same as branding on a ranch. On a ranch, ranchers use branding to differentiate their cattle from every other rancher's cattle (because all cattle look pretty much the same). In the marketplace, branding is what makes a product stand out in a crowd of similar products. The right branding gets you noticed, remembered and sold — or perhaps I should say bought, because today it is all about buying, not selling.

There are four main characteristics of branding that make it an integral part of the marketing and purchasing process.

1. Branding makes you trustworthy and known

Branding makes a product more special than other products. With branding, a normal, everyday product has a personality, and a first and last name, and people know who you are.

In today's marketplace, most products are, more or less, just like their competition. Toilet paper is toilet paper, milk is milk, and a grocery store by any other name is still a grocery store. However, branding takes a product and makes it unique. For example, high-quality drinking water is available from just about every tap in the Western world and it's free, but people pay good money for it when it comes in a bottle. Branding takes bottled water and makes Evian.

Furthermore, every aspect of your brand gives potential customers a feeling or comfort level that they associate with you. The more powerful and positive that feeling is, the more easily and more frequently they will want to do business with you and, indeed, will do business with you.

2. Branding differentiates you from others

Strong branding makes you better than your competition, and makes your product name memorable and easy to remember. Even if your product is absolutely the same as every other product like it, branding makes it special. Branding makes it the first product a consumer thinks about when deciding to make a purchase.

Branding also makes a product seem popular. Everyone knows about it, which implicitly says people like it. And, if people like it, it must be good.

3. Branding makes you worth more money

The stronger your branding is, the more likely people are willing to spend that little bit extra because they believe you, your product, your service, or your business are worth it. They may say they won't, but they will. They do it all the time.

For example, a one-pound box of Godiva chocolates costs about $40; the same weight of Hershey's Kisses costs about $4. The quality of the chocolate isn't ten times greater. The reason people buy Godiva is that the brand Godiva means "gift" whereas the brand Hershey means "snack". Gifts obviously cost more than snacks.

4. Branding pre-sells your product

In the buying age, people most often make the decision on which products to pick up before they walk into the store. The stronger the branding, the more likely people are to think in terms of your product rather than the product category. For example, people are as likely, maybe even more likely, to add Hellmann's to the shopping list as they are to write down simply mayo. The same is true for soda, ketchup, and many other products with successful, strong branding.

Plus, as soon as a shopper gets to the shelf, branding can provide a quick reminder of what products to grab in a few ways:

- An icon or logo
- A specific color
- An audio icon

BRANDING IN A SMALL BUSINESS

Big companies spend millions of dollars on advertising, marketing, and public relations (PR) to build recognition of a new product name. They get their selling messages out to the public using television, radio, magazines, and the Internet. They can even throw money at damage control when necessary. The strategies for branding are the same in a small business, but the scale, costs, and a few of the tactics change.

Make your brand name work harder

The name of a small business can mean everything in terms of branding. Your brand name needs to work harder for your business than you do. It's the first thing a prospective customer sees, and it is how they will remember you. A brand name has to be memorable when spoken, and focused in its meaning. If the name doesn't represent what consumers believe about a product and the company that makes it, then that brand will fail.

In building your product's reputation and image, less is often significantly more. Make sure the name you choose immediately gives a sense of what you do.

Large corporations have millions of dollars to take a meaningless brand name and make it stand for something. Small businesses don't, so use words that really mean something. Strive for something interesting and be right on point. You don't need to be boring.

Plumbers, for example, would do well setting themselves apart with names like "The On-Time Plumber" or "24/7 Plumbing". The same is true for electricians, IT providers, or even marketing consultants. Plenty of other types of business are so general in nature they just don't work hard enough in a business or product name.

Even the playing field: The Net

The Internet has leveled the playing field for small businesses like nothing else. You can use the Internet in several ways to market your brand:

Website: Developing and maintaining a website is easier than ever. Anyone can find your business regardless of its size.

Social Media: Facebook and Twitter can promote your brand in a cost-effective manner.

BUILDING YOUR BRAND WITH THE BRANDING LADDER

Even if you do everything perfectly the first time (and I don't know anyone who does), branding takes time. How much time isn't just up to you, but you can speed things along by understanding the different levels of branding, as well as the business and marketing strategies that can get you to the top.

Introducing the Branding Ladder

Moving through the levels of branding is like climbing a ladder to the top of the marketplace. The Branding Ladder has five distinct rungs and, unlike stairs, you can't take them two at a time. You have to take them in order, and some businesses spend more time on each rung than others.

You can also think of the Branding Ladder in terms of a scale from zero to ten. Everyone starts at zero. If you properly climb the ladder, you can end up at 12 out of 10. The Branding Ladder below shows a special rung at the top of the ladder that can take your business over the top. The following section explains the Branding Ladder and how your small business can move up it.

THE BRANDING LADDER	
Brand Advocacy	12/10
Brand Insistence	10/10
Brand Preference	3/10
Brand Awareness	1/10
Brand Absence	0/10

Rung 1: Living in the void

Your business, in fact every business, starts at the bottom rung, which is called brand absence, meaning you have no brand whatsoever except your own name. On a scale of one to ten, brand absence is, of course, zero. That's the worst place to live and obviously the most difficult entrepreneurially. The good news is that the only way is up.

Ninety-seven percent of businesses live on this rung of the Branding Ladder. They earn far less than they want to earn, far less than they should earn, and far less than they would earn if they did exactly the same work under a real brand.

Rung 2: Achieving awareness

Brand awareness is a good first step up the ladder to the second rung. Actually, it's really good, especially because 97 percent of businesses never get there. You want people to be aware of you. When person A speaks to person B and says, "Have you heard of "The 24/7 Plumber?" You want the answer to be "yes".

On that scale of one to ten, however, brand awareness is only a one. It's better than nothing, but not that much better. Although people know of your brand, being aware doesn't mean that they are interested in buying it. Coca Cola drinkers know about Pepsi, but they don't drink it.

Rung 3: Becoming the preferred brand

Getting to the third rung, brand preference, is definitely a real step up. This rung means that people prefer to use your product or service rather than that of your competition. They believe there is a real difference between you and others, and you're their first choice. This rung is a crucial branding stage for parity products, such as bottled water and breakfast cereals, not to mention plumbers, electricians, lawyers, and all the others. Brand preference is clearly better than brand awareness, but it's less than halfway up the ladder.

Car rental companies represent a perfect example of why brand preference may not be enough. When someone lands at an airport and needs to rent a car on the spot, he or she may go straight to the preferred rental counter. If that company has a car available, it's a sale. However, if all the cars for that company have been rented, the person will move to the next rental kiosk without much thought, because one rental car is just as good as another.

Exerting Brand Preference needs to be easy and convenient

If all you have is brand preference, your business is on shaky ground and you can lose business for the feeblest of reasons. Very few people go to a second or third supermarket just to find their favorite brand of bottled water. Similarly, a shopper may prefer one store over another but, if both stores sell the same products, he or she will often go to the closest store even if it is not the better liked one. The reason for staying nearby does not need to be a dramatic one — the shopper may simply be tired, on a tight schedule, or not in the mood to travel.

Rung 4: Making it you and only you

When your customers are so committed to your product or service that they won't accept a substitute, you have reached the fourth rung of the Branding Ladder. All companies strive to reach this place, called brand insistence.

Brand insistence means that someone's experience with a product in terms of performance, durability, customer service, and image has been sufficiently exceptional. As a result, the product has earned an incredible level of loyalty. If the product isn't available where the customer is, he or she will literally not buy something else. Rather, the person will look for the preferred product elsewhere. Can you imagine what a fabulous place this is for a company to be? Brand insistence is the best of the best, the perfect ten out of ten, the whole ball of wax.

Apple is a perfect example of brand insistence

Apple users don't just think, they know in their heads and hearts, that anything made by Apple is technologically-advanced, user-friendly, and just all-around superior. Committed to everything Apple, Mac users won't even entertain the thought that a PC may have positive attributes.

Apple people love everything about their Macs, iPads, iPhones, the Mac stores and all those apps. When the company introduces a new product, many of its brand-insistent fans actually wait in line overnight to be one of the first to have it. Steve Jobs is one of their idols.

Considering one big potential problem

Unfortunately, you can lose brand insistence much more quickly than you can achieve it. Brand-insistent customers have such high expectations that they can be disillusioned or disappointed by just one bad product experience. You also have to consistently reinforce the positives because insistence can fade over time. Even someone who has bought and re-bought a specific brand of car for the last 20 years can decide it's just time for a change. That's how fickle the world is.

At ten out of ten, brand insistence may seem like the top rung of the ladder, but it's not. One rung is actually better, and it involves getting your brand-insistent customers to keep polishing your brand for you.

Rung 5: Getting customers to do the work for you

Brand advocacy is the highest rung on the ladder. It's better than ten out of ten because you have customers who are so happy with your product that they want everyone to know about it and use it. Think of them as uber-fans. Not only do they recommend you to friends and family, they also practically shout your praises from the rooftops, interrupt conversations among strangers to give their opinion, and tell everyone they meet how fantastic you are. Most companies can only aspire to this level of customer satisfaction. Apple is one of the few large corporations in recent history that has brand advocates all over the world.

- Brand advocacy does the following five extraordinary things for your company. Brand advocacy:

- Provides a level of visibility that you couldn't pay for if you tried. Brand advocates are so enthusiastic they talk about you all the time, and reach people in ways general media and public relations can't. You get great visibility because they make sure people actually listen.

- Delivers free advertising and public relations. Companies love the extra super-positive messaging, all for free.

- Affords a level of credibility that literally can't be bought. Brand advocates are more than just walking testimonials. They are living proof that you are the best.

- Provides pre-sold prospective customers. Advocate recommendations carry so much weight that they are worth much more than plain referrals. They deliver customers ready and committed to purchasing your product or service.

- Increases profits exponentially. Brand advocates are money-making machines for your business because they increase sales and decrease marketing costs.

For these reasons, brand advocacy is 12 out of 10!!

BRANDING YOURSELF: HOW TO DO SO IN FOUR EASY WAYS

If you're interested in branding your product or company, you may not be sure where to begin. The good news: I'm here to help. You can brand in many ways, but here I pare it down to four ways to help you start:

Branding by association

This way involves hanging out with and being seen with people who are very much higher than you in your particular niche.

Branding by achievement

This way repurposes your previous achievements.

Branding by testimonial

This way makes use of the testimonials that you receive but have likely never used.

Branding by WOW

A WOW is the pleasantly unexpected, the equivalent of going the extra mile. The easiest and most certain way to WOW people is to tell them that you've written a book. To discover how you can write a book, go to www.BrandingSmallBusinessForDummies.com.

Sex, Love and Relationships

DR. JOHN GRAY

Just as great sex is important to lasting love, good health is important to sex and relationships. About 12 years ago, I cured myself of early stage Parkinson's disease. The doctors were amazed, but my wife was even more amazed. She noted that our relationship and sex life had become dramatically better. It turns out that the natural supplements I used to reverse Parkinson's can also make you more attentive and loving in your relationship. At that point, I realized that good relationship skills alone were not enough to sustain love and passion for a lifetime.

I shared many insights gained from my 40 years' experience as a marriage counselor and coach in *Men Are From Mars, Women Are From Venus*. And while my insights go a long way towards helping men and women understand and support each other, good communication skills alone are not always enough. For better relationships, we not only need to be healthy, but we must also experience optimum brain function.

If you are tired, depressed, anxious, not sleeping well, or in pain, then certainly romantic feelings will become a thing of the past. My recovery from Parkinson's revealed to me the profound connection between the quality of our health and our relationships. This insight has motivated me, over the past twelve years, to research the secrets of optimum health as a foundation for lasting love.

These are health secrets that are generally not explored in medical school. In medical school, doctors are indoctrinated into the culture of examining the symptoms, identifying the sickness, and prescribing a drug to treat that sickness. They learn very little about how to be healthy or to sustain successful relationships.

There are no university courses entitled "Better Nutrition For Better Sex". Drugs sometimes save lives, but they also have negative side effects that do little to preserve the passion in a relationship. Ideally, drugs should be used as a last resort and 90 % of our health plan should be drug free. From this perspective, the heath care crisis, as well as our high rate of divorce in America, is indirectly caused by our dependence on doctors and prescription drugs.

Most people have not even considered that taking prescribed drugs (even for the small stuff) can weaken their relationships, which in turn makes them more vulnerable to more disease. For example, if you are feeling depressed or anxious, a drug may numb your pain, but it does nothing to help you correct the cause of your problem. It can even prevent you from feeling your natural motivation to get the emotional support you need. In a variety of ways, our common health complaints are all expressions of two major conditions: our lack of education to identify and support unmet gender-specific emotional needs; and our lack of education to identify and support unmet gender-specific nutritional needs.

With an understanding of natural solutions that have been around for thousands of years, drugs are not needed to treat many common complaints. Some symptoms like low energy, weight gain, allergies, hormonal imbalance, mood swings, poor sleep, indigestion, lack of focus, ADD and ADHD, procrastination, low motivation, memory loss, decreased libido, PMS, vaginal dryness, muscle and joint pain, or the lack of passion in life and/or our relationships can be treated drug-free. By using drugs (even over-the-counter drugs) to treat these common complaints, our bodies and relationships are weakened, making us more vulnerable to bigger and more costly health challenges like cancer, diabetes, heart disease, auto-immune disease, dementia, and Alzheimer's. In simple terms, by handling the easy stuff (the common complaints) without doctors and drugs, we can protect ourselves from the big stuff (cancer, heart disease, dementia, etc.) We can be healthy and also enjoy lasting love and passion in our personal lives.

Even if you are taking anti-depressants or hormone replacement therapy, sometimes all it takes to stop treating the symptom is to directly handle the cause. With specific mineral orotates (something most people have never heard of) or omega three oil from the brains of salmon, your stress levels immediately drop and you begin to feel happy and in love again.

For every health challenge, we have explored the effects on our relationships, with as well as natural remedies that can sometimes produce immediate positive results. You can find these natural solutions to common health complaints for free at my website: www.MarsVenus.com.

What they don't teach in medical school is how to be healthy and happy without the use of drugs or hormone replacement. By refusing drugs and taking responsibility for your health, a wealth of new possibilities can become available to you. We are designed to be healthy and happy, and it is within our reach if we commit to increasing our knowledge.

New research regarding the brain differences in men and women reveals how specific nutritional supplements, combined with gender-specific relationship and self-nurturing skills, can stimulate the hormones of health, happiness and increased energy. Over the past 10 years in my healing center in California, I witnessed how natural solutions coupled with gender-specific relationship skills could solve our common health complaints without drugs. By addressing these common complaints without prescribed drugs, not only do we feel better, but our relationships have the potential to improve dramatically.

Ultimately the cause of all our common complaints is higher stress levels. Researchers around the world all agree that chronic stress levels in our bodies provide a basis for any and all disease to take hold. An easy and quick solution for lowering our stress reactions is specific nutritional support combined with gender-smart relationship skills. Extra nutritional support is needed because stress depletes the body very quickly of essential nutrients. When a car engine is running more quickly, it uses fuel more quickly. When we are stressed, we need both extra nutrients and extra emotional support. Understanding what we need to take and where to get it requires education. Every week day at www.MarsVenus.com I have a live daily show where I freely answer questions and provide this much-needed new gender-specific insight.

At www.MarsVenus.com, we are happy to share what we have learned for creating healthy bodies and positive relationships. You can find a host of natural solutions for common complaints and feel confident that you have the power to feel fully alive with an abundance of energy and positive feelings that will enrich all your relationships.

The Secret
to Words

JACQUELINE LUCIEN

When you first learned to read, you probably were taught to associate each letter with an object and a sound. It was pretty flat-footed, like "A" is for apple or "B" is for ball. The things your parents or teachers used to illustrate the sound represented by each letter may have made sense to you? Did you ever wonder what the letters originally stood for, *or if they stood for anything* or how someone came up with their specific shapes and curves?

Each letter we use today has a rich and fascinating, multi-layered meaning. Each has a history of associations that make it just about perfect in terms of its shape and design. Just like Chinese and Japanese characters, each letter of the alphabet represents so much more than just a sound — it tells a story and conveys the ancient and original meaning in a powerful way which influences our words today. So, how did these letters that mean so much in our daily lives come to be in the first place?

We all know the old saying that a picture is worth a thousand words. Well, it's true and nowhere more so than when talking about the letters we use to read and write. The alphabet is connected to ancient pictures, and the essence of those pictures comes from both concrete objects and abstract ideas. If a picture is worth a thousand words, and letters (in their ancient essence) are pictures, *what is the worth of one letter? What is the worth of one word?*

THE CREATION OF THE ROMAN ALPHABET

The Roman alphabet (the 26 letters from A to Z used to create the English language) originated in Ancient Egypt. (The Romans influenced, and were influenced, by many cultures.) The Egyptian form of writing is called *"Mdu Ntr," Medu Neter or the hieroglyphics of KMT, which means the Language of the Gods.* The characters, sometimes called ideographs, pictographs or phonograms, are symbols or pictures used to represent sounds or words. From these Ancient Egyptian hieroglyphs, letters were created. Each letter shape can be traced back to a hieroglyph, and the hieroglyph itself (or its meaning) can be directly connected to the way in which we use that letter on a daily basis.

How wonderful it would be for me to regale you with a story about the origin of each of our 26 Roman letters, but that would take a whole book — and that is something for another time. Instead, let's focus on the Roman letters A, B, D, and P, as well as the connection between the Gods and letters "G" and "N." The origins of these letters range from simple to complex, and provide a broad view of how the Roman alphabet came to be.

A IS FOR "APED/VULTURE

It is fairly safe to say that the letter "A" is one of, if not, the first letter children learn. As I mentioned, it is highly likely that a child first learns "A is for apple". What that child doesn't get taught is that "A" stands for lots of other things that actually better relate to the letter itself. After all, an A is a high reaching letter coming to a point; a round apple looks nothing like an A.

In ancient times, for example, a child might have been told "A is for aped." The Egyptian word "aped" is represented by a hieroglyph of a bird; and translates to the scientific word for bird (more specifically, vulture). The vulture ("aped") has a bad reputation these days, but was originally known for being a high-flying bird that valiantly cared for its young. The aped was also considered the Pharaoh's favorite bird. Clearly, the aped had a high station in the culture, making it a great choice for the first letter of the alphabet.

Digging deeper, let's look at the qualities represented by the letter A itself, and how those qualities are related to the aped. The A is reminiscent of pyramids; it is a triangle with great heights. Further, the aped is linked to words like "Air"… "Altitude"… "Ascend" … "Appreciate" — words that all have meanings connected to greatness, height and direction. These words' meanings, coupled with the fact that the letter A is represented by a distinct and greatly appreciated bird, are all indicators of why the capital letter A itself is visually tall and reminiscent of height.

There is a second 'glyph' represented by an arm, thus the word arm. And, for example, it is the "a" in leverage. Thus, one would have to make a distinction between which glyph is represented in the word in question. This will be elaborated further in my book, along with many other examples.

Further, the great Egyptian God Amun, an incredibly influential and powerful God, is later called "Amen," the same word used by many religions to end a prayer. The importance of the A is so great that it is used, in part, to finalize the hopes and thoughts of multitudes of people to ensure that they are heard and responded to by their equivalent of the great Egyptian God Amun. Jumping ahead, Amun is an ascended / high and wise/seeing god.

B IS FOR BARE FOOT

In continuing with our exploration into letter origins, let's look at the letter "B". It originates from the hieroglyph of a bare foot. Among the first qualities we can associate with a bare foot is down (or downward) as the bare foot is at the bottom, or base, of the body. (Can you see a pattern emerging?) The bare foot is support for the body, like a brace or the base of a table. The bare foot helps with movement, bringing you to where you need to be. "Bottom"… "Base"… "Brace"… "Bring"… These words indicate support in both stillness and movement.

The letter B itself is sturdy. The bottom, larger than the top, stabilizes the letter, holding the letter upright, just as the bare foot holds up the rest of the body. When we look at the shape of the lowercase "b," we see its appearance is very similar to that of a leg and barefoot. Other examples of how the letter shows up in our language include: "Boots on the ground" and "Battalion," both representing foot soldiers.

D IS FOR DIGITS /HAND

The letter "D" originated from the hieroglyphic symbol of a hand. The Egyptian word for hand is drrt , The function of the hand (because of our opposable thumbs) separates man from the animals. Man does many things with his hand(s). Among the words that start with D, and are connected to the hieroglyph, is the word "digits," i.e., the fingers of the hand. Digits help man "Do" things... "Duty"... "Drive"... "Diligence." These words are all connected to man doing and accomplishing something. Even more closely linked to the letter D and the hieroglyph of the hand are words such as "dexterous" and "dexterity." The meanings of these words are directly related to hands and the ability of the hand to perform tasks. Thus, D has the quality of action and is directly related to the action of the hand. *Even though the English word hand does not start with the letter d its meaning is consistent in the word.*

☐ P IS FOR PORTAL/DOOR

You may be wondering why I chose to jump all the way to "P" at this point. It's because of the very interesting connection between two letters that I want to share with you. The Egyptian hieroglyph for "P" is a square, more specifically, a door. Now, think about the letter D again. If you were to turn the lowercase letter "d" around (by 180 degrees), what would you have? Yes! A small letter "p"! The d in the picture of the door that we see in the hieroglyph is truly a p, as in the word "Portal." I also looked across languages in Spanish you have puerta.

While it might not be your first thought, when considering doors or portals, we are truly thinking of going out into an open space or a place that affords opportunity (opportunity having the double-p, or two portals... even the word "port" is embedded in "opportunity"). The letter P is instrumental in many common sayings, including, "When opportunity knocks, answer the door" and "window of opportunity." These sayings allude to the double-p (two portals) in opportunity, and the door or portal at which to respond to the opportunity being given to you. So the quality of a door to be considered is that it is an opening, something you can go through. The words that come to mind are: passage...privilege...progress....port....peer (as in look through).

THE LETTERS OF THE GODS

A deeper analysis of letters and hieroglyphs reveals the remarkable way in which some letters correlate with the ancient Gods worshipped by the Egyptians. To appreciate the connection between the two you need to know a bit about Egyptian Cosmology.

Cosmology in general is the study of origins and the universe. Egyptian cosmology revolves around the required balance between humans and the Gods. Humans believed that if they were cooperative, kind and just to one another, the Gods would, in turn, be kind and keep the forces of nature in balance. There are many Gods in Egyptian Cosmology: The God of the ground/earth (Geb), the God of the night/sky (Goddess Nut), the God of the sun (Re), the God of air (Shu) and the God of chaos (Nu). I'm going to focus on the first two Gods, Geb and Nut, for the next part of our journey through the alphabet.

⟁ G IS FOR "GEB

The letter "G" comes from the hieroglyphic letter or symbol for the stool. In this respect, the stool is defined as a stand upon which you put a jar. That definition suggests support, foundation, and a most telling word, "grounding" (the stool is on the ground). The "G" also represents the Egyptian God, Geb. As previously mentioned, Geb is the God of earth itself. Egyptian cosmology states that Geb is quite literally the earth... the "ground"... the "geography"... the "globe". The earth "gives" and supports life. The earth "grows; "it generates." As a result, it makes perfect sense for the letter "G" to come out of a symbol that represents an object that grounds and supports, and is the foundation for other objects and beings. Geb is also shown supporting or holding up Nut, the night/sky. Geb is Nut's husband/brother. Does that give you something to consider regarding the ancient wisdom for the need to support?

ᐱᐱᐱᐱ N IS FOR NUT

The letter "N" originated from the hieroglyph of wavy lines, similar to waves and water. Some say that N represents water, which is a source of life. Also, similar to the letter G, the Roman letter N is connected to both Egyptian hieroglyphs and the Egyptian Gods.

In Egyptian Cosmology, there is the Goddess Nut. She gave birth to the sun, and the sun revolves around her body in a 24-hour cycle to make night and day. Nut is commonly depicted as a woman who is arched over the earth (Geb) on hands and feet. The Goddess Nut is representative of the barrier between chaos and the cosmos and is seen as a protector of the dead whom she keeps with her in her starry sky.

The Goddess Nut is the night, the darkness from which everything derives. In English, she is the "Night". In Spanish, she is the "Noche"... in French "Nuit"... in Greek "Nyx" ... Nacht in German ... "Nox" in Latin ... in Sanskrit "Naktam" and in Hindi "Nishaa."

"Nyx" (Ancient Greek: Νυξ, "night")" in the Latin translation is the Greek goddess, or personification, of the night. A shadowy figure, Nyx stood at or near the beginning of creation and was the mother of other personified Gods such as Hypnos (Sleep) and Thánatos (Death). Nyx's appearances in mythology are few and far between, but what has been revealed about her is that she is a figure of exceptional power and beauty. Nyx is found in the shadows of the world and is only ever seen in glimpses. As you get away from the source, the object or concept can gain other interpretations.

When we see the reference to Nut as protector of death, it represents that, as time went on, words that were powerful from the opposite quality. The words that come to mind are Engish "no" … Spanish "nada," …german "nicht", " nein"

I urge you to continue with your own exploration of the word "night", its spellings and meanings across languages. It is unlikely that the Gods from one belief system to the next can be so similar in both names and existence without it being anything less than purposeful.

So… what does all of this Goddess Nut and Night talk have to do with the Roman letter N? Well, the letter N is derived directly from Nut. And, again, Nut is the night, a bringer of life (like the water depicted in the hieroglyph), and the protector of the dead. Nut's role is natural and nurturing. Nut is the N in origin, beginning, expansive and garden. She is the N in neuter, as she was disempowered through time and forgotten for her role as giving birth to the son. And, what about the word "not" representing further neutralization and negation? As you look at how she is depicted, with her arching body, you can see she is the N in expansive beginning and origin. She is also the N in the words span and extend over or across something, like space and time.

The capital letter N looks physically similar to the waves in the hieroglyph.

Interestingly, the depiction of Nut in her arched form is also similar in shape to the lowercase Roman "n". These connections between Roman letters, hieroglyphs, and Ancient Egyptian Gods cannot be ignored or thrown aside. These connections are very much real.

Ok, I Can See It. But Why Should I Care?

While reading thus far, have you said to yourself, "this may be interesting, but how can I use this information?" Or, are you thinking that this chapter satisfies a little curiosity, but that's it; you'll move on to something else because this information does not have any real purpose for you. How can you actually use this in your life?

Doesn't this understanding of letters make them seem so much more alive? Have you not gained a greater appreciation for the letters we use to construct our most meaningful of words? Consider for just a moment how much more enlightening the learning of the Roman alphabet could be to a five-year-old child if he or she were taught by way of hieroglyphics, meaning and origin. The very nature of learning would be greatly enhanced.

Children would not only learn what each hieroglyphic and Roman letter looks like, but would also understand their meanings. Learning the origin of each letter provides the opportunity to more fully grasp the how and why of each shape and sound, as well as the connection of these shapes and sounds to the bigger piece – reading words as a whole. Further, understanding each letter's origin enhances the learning of vocabulary and spelling by making connections with the meaning of letters and the purpose each holds within a word. The more we use our five senses to learn, the more mastery we can have. *Children could be encouraged to put letters together to create their own words, another form of creativity and another way to tell their story. I invite you to consider additional uses for this information.*

BUT I'M BEYOND LEARNING TO READ

Pictures provide a very profound way to anchor learning and memory. Further, pictures and words, particularly when they work together, are exceptionally useful tools for drawing you in to a subject. Graphic artists are taught to come up with abstract ideas and create logos to convey meaning, (the same thought process used to create the hieroglyphics) while advertisers use words and pictures to gain access to your mind and influence your perception.

As an example, let's talk about the soda 7UP®. Would the brand name affect you the same way if it were 7b? (The b that is downward and associated with the bare foot.) No, of course it wouldn't, because, in its essence, 7b is a "downer." So, instead, we are sold 7UP, which includes the letter P associated with an upward door, an opening and an *opportunity* for something. The brand name 7UP is pure genius. Without the understanding and purpose of our letters, we are unable to understand the cause and effect of what we are seeing.

Also, by unlocking the meaning of letters, you can cross check the dictionary or encyclopedia and go beyond the history of the words, the etymology to understand how letters and words interact with each other. What are the letters really saying? Why is it that a word can mean something in one language, but mean something completely different in another language? When you explore the reference tools I just mentioned, you see that the meaning of a word changes according to the culture and powers that be at the time. Now you have the tools to see how the story of the letters supports the dictionary meaning, or not, and why.

Learning occurs in stages; since this is an introduction I chose words to represent the concepts presented, primarily having the letter at the beginning of the word. Once there is a command of the concept you begin to see its function in any part of the word.

Further, we can empower children by providing them with an understanding of the meanings and origins of the letters in their names. We can challenge them to personify each letter and gain strength, courage and leadership skills based on the history associated with their names. The big picture impact is that we can teach children to read and write with this new perspective. We can use the origin and meaning of letters to create logos and company names that are more powerful and impactful than ever before. We can provide another efficient way to remember names by seeing what the letters in the name say. We can advance into the future by using the keys provided by our world's ancient history and earliest writing.

If you would like more information about hieroglyphics in general, or want to learn more about the meaning of a specific letter or word, like your name, please feel free to contact me at jahkey2@gmail.com .

Outshine the Competition: Coming Out on Top in the Interview Process

OSSY BOTHA

"Sometimes one creates a dynamic impression by saying something, and sometimes one creates as significant an impression by remaining silent."

– The Dalai Lama

Interview Dynamics introduces a concept which helps Career & Job Seekers prepare, refine and polish the "how & what" in any interview situation; how to describe and what to say about their skills and experiences. - Ossy

There are no two ways about it. Job-hunting in today's harsh economic realities is tougher than ever before. If the prospect of job interviews sends shivers up and down your spine, you're not alone. Global expansion and outsourcing, technological innovation and a spate of economic crises have changed the employment landscape beyond recognition, and a job-seeker is stepping into an unknown that few have wandered into before. In short, nailing the interview is much more of a priority than ever before.

There are new rules when it comes to looking for a job, and it's no longer just about possessing the right resumé. Whether you are fresh out of college, changing careers or wanting a promotion in your current company or current field, you have to go through an interview, come across as a credible candidate, and then show you are the best fit for the job. You have to deliver a flawless performance while juggling the stresses of applying for several jobs at the same time. It's a tremendous burden to bear, and it's no surprise that many applicants cringe at the thought of readying themselves for an interview. There are loads of how-to books on the shelves in bookstores and libraries, many of them filled with theory, tips and advice -- none of which you'll remember in the heat of an interview.

So, how do you really get up to speed to out-prepare and outshine the competition? The solution is quite simple. We help you gain the confidence and the assuredness you need so that, rather than stepping into the interview with clammy palms and nervous tics, you'll breeze in with a confident stride, a smile on your face and a strong handshake, and come out a winner.

WHAT IS INTERVIEW DYNAMICS AND ITS PURPOSE?

Each one of us performs various roles in our lives. You are a brother, son, boyfriend, colleague, uncle, husband or a mother, daughter, BFF, stepsister, aunt and so on. You take on the roles that are expected of you without question and switch from being parent to sibling in the blink of an eye.

Similarly, as a work colleague we take on our different profiles while we perform the various roles applicable to our job criteria, whether we are the Office Cleaner or the CEO.

In the office, you are a colleague and, simultaneously, a department head. You have to report to a board of several bosses and, at the same time, have to take care of several junior employees. You have to motivate the ranks below you, you have to sell new ideas to your bosses and you have to take care of all the paperwork! Basically, you wear several hats at work and, during the course of a workday, you move seamlessly from one role to another.

In Interview Dynamics, we help you to do the same. We teach you to think of yourself as a business, and we remove the personal ego from the preparation. The brutal truth is that, no matter how qualified you may be, there is always the possibility of someone more highly skilled than yourself. You can bone up as much as you can by reading books on interviewing, rehearsing your answers and doing your homework, but it's how you fare during your interview that seals your fate.

So, rather than have you present yourself as a nervous candidate, we take you step-by-step through the practicalities of preparing for an interview. We guide you through several processes and we help you change your mindset. There are many books on interviewing skills and they advocate that you brush up on your strengths and weaknesses, but do they tell you how to do just that?

When I was coaching a client through Interview Dynamics, I asked her to tell me about a mistake she had made at work. She was totally flabbergasted by the question and several awkward minutes ticked by and she still couldn't come up with an answer. Luckily, this was a practice run, and she subsequently used the tools in Interview Dynamics to prepare herself for the real thing.

We build your confidence through shifting your perspective in order to tap the infinite resources that already reside within you and to leverage the skills inherent in you to suit the occasion. The simple truth is that you are a multi-talented person and, rather than presenting yourself as a one-dimensional candidate to the employer, how about viewing yourself as a business which we call Firm You (Pty) Ltd?

This company, Firm You, has a range of services and products, namely your work experience, credentials and other qualities such as leadership, communication and motivational skills that will greatly benefit the end-consumer of the company you are interviewing with. In return for supplying these "goods and services", you are paid money, as you would in any business transaction, in the form of a salary.

Residing within you, waiting to be called to the fore, are several important figures of authority in the business – the Managing Director, the Financial Director, the Sales Director and the Project Director. Depending on the task at hand during the interview, you will wear the hat that most suits the role you are playing. For example, during that phase of interview when you have to persuade the (slightly skeptical) interviewer that you're the best person for the job, you bring forth the Sales Director of Firm You, because he or she is the best suited for this particular task.

Let's take a pause and try this idea on for size. Let's pretend that you are the Sales Director of a very successful company named Firm You. You're present at a meeting selling a business or service. You are not a single person. Instead, you are a business that contains a multitude of talents, skills and viewpoints.

Can you see how this change in perspective takes the sting of anxiety and stress out of the interviewing process? Can you feel the shift that takes place within when you re-imagine the process as a sales meeting, not a nerve-wracking interview? That, in simple terms, is the essence of Interview Dynamics.

We take you through various exercises that are the cornerstones of Interview Dynamics. Each of them is meant to prepare you so thoroughly that you'll be ready with an answer to any question that is thrown at you during the interview. The cornerstones of Interview Dynamics are: -

1. Knowing yourself
2. Projecting yourself with confidence and communicating with clarity
3. The Business Plan

We briefly mentioned the various figures of authority within Firm You; now let's take a closer look at what each of them encompasses before explaining how they kick in during the interview process.

THE ASSETS THAT LIE WITHIN

To recap, Firm You (Pty) Ltd is You. The company you are hoping to land a job in is a potential customer called the Prospective Employer.

There are four important job designations within Firm You: -

1. Managing Director – The MD is the visionary who, through investment in education, training and work experience, has guided Firm You to where it is today. As MD, he or she wants to direct the business to the next level.

2. Financial Director – He or she knows the value of your business (or your salary) and must have this figure at his or her fingertips in order to arrive at a fair deal during negotiations with the prospective employer.

3. Sales Director – The Sales Director is always on the ball. For the Sales Director, an interview is just another business meeting. He or she is the public face of Firm You, and is always "selling" on the job during the daily course of work. Let's not mistake "selling" with just being words and fluff and little else. Firm You has to back up the sales pitch of the Sales Director with a solid, outstanding performance.

4. Project Director - He or she is the one who goes all out into doing the research and the homework. The Project Director delves into the ins and outs of a potential job – analyzing the job description, the tasks and projects that make up the job, the skills, training and education required – all with the goal of matching your assets and qualifications to the job description. By verifying all that is required for the position, you can clearly show how you are able to deliver.

BUILDING THE BUSINESS OF FIRM YOU

We start with you wearing the hat of a Project Director who, in a manner of speaking, has to draft out a blueprint for a major project. Imagine a project director tasked with bidding for a project to build a bridge. He or she has to identify the assets and resources available, pinpoint strengths, weaknesses and experience of such resources, organize them into various functional teams, identify key tasks and lay out a timeline.

In this case, you're the Project Director and Firm You is your task at hand. There are three steps that you have to undertake:

- Task A: Brainstorm and jot down all your skills, experiences, extra training, your problem-solving expertise, and strengths and weaknesses relevant to the position you are applying for. This is a no-holds barred session; let go, write down everything that comes to mind. Don't edit yourself -- that comes later. At this stage, use as many pages as you need.

- Task B: Organize the mass of information from Task A into distinct categories relevant to the functions in the job description. Categories include education, skills, competencies, tasks, projects, jobs functions and so forth. This continues until all information from Task A has been neatly slotted under the various appropriate headings.

- Task C: Chunk up information from Task 2 and extract only key tasks appropriate to each heading. This is the final step in your homework as Project Director. You take only the most relevant information from each of the categories in Task B and transfer them to another page with the following important headings: education, courses, tech-skills, job functions, strengths and weaknesses, salary, questions about the job. Think of this as the final step in connecting the dots between what you have and what is required.

KNOW YOURSELF:
COMMUNICATION + CLARIFICATION + COMMUNICATION

These next exercises are to get you to thoroughly know yourself. By working through the three tasks from A to C, you are building and re-familiarizing yourself with a database of resources, competencies and skills that you already have at your disposal. Through this exercise, you'll regain confidence in who you really are and refresh your memory as to your creativity, achievements and accomplishments.

During the interview, you'll be wearing the hat of the Sales Director, who is out to sell the business of Firm You (Pty) Ltd. Having done this kind of homework, you'll be able to answer difficult and awkward questions with credibility and authority, and basically demonstrate that you have all it takes to land the job.

Having all the important bits of information at your fingertips because of the hard work put into preparation, you, as the Sales Director, are able to communicate clearly.

You will also be in a position of strength to answer with clarity, without hemming or hawing or taking awkward pauses, any questions the interviewer may ask of you.

Lastly, you will come across as a confident figure because you are well-prepared; you are able to adroitly handle any awkward questions thrown at you on any aspect of the job at hand.

REMUNERATION

You have come this far in the interview process, and now you could come undone in what is inevitably a sticky issue: how much you should be paid. No matter how well you have performed so far, this issue could be the deal-breaker if you don't put sufficient thought into your worth.

In Interview Dynamics, we provide a different take on this subject. We give you a formula, one coined by your Financial Director (it's now his or her time to step up to the plate), so you can reframe the salary negotiation not as a do-or-die situation, but as a means of getting a fair return on your output.

When you think about it, you strike a deal with someone who sells you a product or service because you think and feel you're getting a fair return on your money. Let's take this point a little further. Your Prospective Employer buys from Firm You and pays you in the form of your salary (Total Cost to Company or TCTC), in order to get desirable products and services to sell to his end customer in return for money. Naturally, he will want to make a profit on top of this cost. In order for the Prospective Employer to make a fair return and to strike a deal with you, your Financial Director values Firm You as follows: -

TCTC X 4 = Your Salary X 1 + TCTC X 3 = Profit to Prospective Employer = Fair Deal.

FROM PREP TO THE DOTTED LINE: SO WHO ARE YOU?

Now that we've covered the groundwork, there's still a little way to go before you get to sign on the dotted line. You have to be comfortable talking about yourself and polishing your storytelling skills. The more success stories you can offer, the better you show yourself as being likely to achieve equivalent success in the future. You have to be able to talk about yourself because, without fail, the question will come up "Tell us about yourself." You're certainly not boosting your hiring chances if you hesitate or respond with something unprofessional like "What do you wish to know?"

With that in mind, you have to be fully prepared to talk in detail about work that you have done in the past that made a difference to your then employer. As part of our process in Interview Dynamics, we'll guide you to coming up with concrete examples such as how you successfully closed a sale with an important customer or how you found solutions to an ongoing and expensive problem. Be conversant with your strengths and weaknesses to help your interviewer connect the dots as to why you are a winning pick for the job. This phase of the process is not as tough as it sounds because of all the prep work previously done by your Project Director.

Being asked about your mistakes is a normal thing. Do not panic, because it is in fact something that you can prepare for. Take the time right now to consider what you have done wrong. As you talk about the incident, talk about how you fixed it, how you learned from it, and how you would prevent something like that from ever happening again! This shows initiative, and it also gives your Prospective Employer an idea of how you could solve any of their problems in the future.

THE BUSINESS PLAN

Now, you turn the spotlight on the job itself. Is this project worth bidding for, so to speak? Does the job in question meet your needs? In a manner of speaking, Firm You has to analyze this opportunity, just as any business considering a potential investment would, and thus come up with a business plan. As Project Director, you have done the research and crunched the analytics. The Managing Director then weighs up whether or not this new job will take Firm You and its profitability to the next level. The Financial Director suggests the price that Firm You wants and, if everyone is in agreement, it is then up to the Sales Director to sell Firm You.

QUESTIONING THE QUESTIONER

As the interview process winds down, you may feel that you are in the home stretch. However, there is still the area where you are allowed to ask the person giving the interview any questions you have in mind. Make no mistake about it -- this is as much a test as anything else that has transpired before.

In the previous part of the interview, you were being tested to see how well you responded to stimuli. Now you are being judged on how well you are able to act independently.

Remember that, if you have done your research about the company and have the business plan at hand, you have plenty to talk about. For example, if you have noticed that the company has been very active on social media, mention it and ask if there are responsibilities, considering your ease at social marketing, which you can cover. This shows initiative, and it also allows the questioner to see how interested you are in the job.

You may choose to ask what they feel the biggest challenge of the job will be. Not only will this give you some very important information about the job, you'll also discover that it gives you a chance to tell them how you would deal with it.

Do not allow the space in the interview where you are allowed to ask questions catch you by surprise. They are watching for that because this is where many people show how unprepared or unsuitable they are. For example, if you are interviewing at a non-profit organisation and, suddenly, all you can talk about are vacation days, there's likely a mismatch there!

Do not miss out on this great opportunity to show your prospective employers how interested you are in what they do. This isn't a time when the tables are turned. In fact, it is just a shift in the form of the interview. They are still looking at you, and you still need to impress them!

FINALIZING THE INTERVIEW DYNAMICS PROCESS

Reading is all well and good, but now you need to put some physical effort into the process. With all of this preparation, which is integral throughout Interview Dynamics, you have all the raw information that you need to make a great impression at your interview. Now you need to refine it, and that starts with writing.

Whether you are most comfortable with a pen and pencil, or you are someone who is most at ease in front of a computer screen, you are now going to sit down and put your interviewing skills and writing skills to work.

Sit down, clear your head and start typing up the interview as you imagine it happening to you. Write out all of the questions that you think will be asked, and spend some time with each one. What do you think they are asking you, and what do you think they are looking for? Then, using this information, craft your responses.

Some people balk at writing line-by- line responses. They fear that it will feel rehearsed or simply trite, but the truth of the matter is that it is not as though you will be reading these things out loud to the person who is interviewing you! Instead, writing out your response will give you a strong foundation on which you can build your answers. You will know the content of what you want to say, but as the situation develops and as you gain more confidence and more mastery over what is going on, you will simply be using the original groundwork as a springboard to the right answer.

When you are preparing to sell yourself to a prospective buyer, you will find that one of the most important things that you can do is to be prepared. Once you have the information that you need, go over it again and again until you know it completely. You may think that you know your strengths and your weaknesses but, until you have been over them a few times, you will never be able to explain them to others.

Good preparation is the key to success and, not only must you have the abilities that the employer is asking for, you must also be someone who can talk about them and who can make the employer understand what you are offering. Do not fall behind simply because, after all the preparation you have done, you fall down on the delivery!

A PROFESSIONAL APPLICATION

It can often feel as if you are walking a fine line between presenting yourself as a unique individual and standing out for being too silly or too personal but, with Interview Dynamics, we show you how to walk that line with absolutely no fear at all. When you think about the fact that there may be dozens, perhaps even hundreds or thousands, of people applying for the job that you want, it is natural to get cold feet but, by applying the principles of Interview Dynamics, you have the advantage of a strong foundation to fall back on.

We show you how to create a rock-solid presentation for your application, and it is founded upon sheer professionalism. A resumé and an application get your foot in the door at the place where you want to work, but being able to demonstrate that you have a lot to bring to the table and that you have what it takes will send your name right to the top of the candidate list.

The key is to leave your ego out of it. You have done many things in your life, and you have certainly done things to be proud of. You have conquered mountains and of course you are proud of the effort that you have put in. However, the thing to remember is that the business that is speaking to you is not interested as much in how hard you work, but in seeing the results that you produce.

This is the key to professionalism and one that few people really grasp. In the quest to learn more about the business that you want to work with, get to know them. What results are they looking for? Do they want their company name to be known as a leader in green initiatives? Are they looking to make sure that they always come out on top in their field? Are they hoping to reform an image that might have been tarnished or dented in recent years?

If you want to make your application stand out, remember that it is less about you and more about the people with whom you are trying to communicate. There has never been a better time to be you, and you must show the company that you are considering why that might be.

Leave your ego at the door, and remember that your application needs to show them why they not only want you, but why they need you!

TAKING SCORE AND PRESENTING THE SALES PITCH

We are now almost at the end of the process. Just to make sure all your bases are covered, we'll score all the prep work you have done to identify what may be missing and what may need to be further supplemented. Once you're satisfied with the score, we'll move on to the last section.

As the final step, we'll run you through a self-interview where you ask questions of yourself and write down your answers to take a measure of how effectively your Sales Director is pitching your business. Are you selling your business in an efficient and professional manner? Where do you need to be refined and polished? What more do you need to know? Are you fully prepared to proceed and come through with flying colors?

By presenting yourself as a business, you are in fact able to distance yourself from the personal anxieties and insecurities that often dog an interview. Instead, you are selling a business you believe in – Firm You – and by doing so you are separating yourself from the sea of applicants and showing up as a winner!

There are multiple uses of Interview Dynamics. It is not just a process to get a new job. You can use all the steps embodied in Interview Dynamics to perform a self-assessment of your work before your annual review or, if you are lobbying for a promotion, use this same process to clearly establish why you deserve better, what additional skills and competencies you have to offer, how you have sought to improve yourself throughout the year, and how the company is going to get a fair value for your services. This process works for anyone, whether you are reporting to the financial director who answers to the board of directors or whether you are an office clerk reporting to the office manager.

Remember, you may not always be the best candidate with the most premium skills. But if you come across as being fully prepared and fully confident, you will be the most memorable and very likely the most winning candidate.

I wish you every success in selling Firm You (Pty) Ltd.

Hi, my name is Ossy Botha. I am from Johannesburg South Africa where I've worked in the recruitment industry for 32 years and counting.

Over this period of time, I have recruited and placed people in various positions and in many different companies – both large and small.

The positions which I recruit for cover a wide range of disciplines -- from senior management level to office support, administration, sales, logistics, production, technical support personnel and the like.

In a nutshell, from the front door receptionist to the back door of the business and from the bottom to the top floor.

Throughout the years, I have attended many courses, read articles on interviewing skills and gained interview techniques from the internet, all of which have proven to be very helpful.

The Interview Dynamics concept is vastly different from any existing techniques. In fact, I have not come across any material that remotely resembles what Interview Dynamics has to offer.

The reason for incorporating Interview Dynamics into your preparation is that it is a deep and thorough process during which you really get to know yourself while gaining tools and skills on how to represent yourself during an interview.

Interview Dynamics changes your perception from an applicant hoping to land the job, to that of a Company Director attending a business meeting.

Over the past years I have interviewed a countless number of people with whom I have shared the Interview Dynamics concept, all of whom have been grateful for receiving this methodology.

Therefore, I would like to share this accolade received from Savashni who was applying for a local and overseas creditor's administrator position. After our initial discussion, I walked her through the Interview Dynamics methodology.

Unfortunately, she was not invited to the prospective employer for an interview because they had just offered the opportunity to another applicant whom I had introduced to the company simply because she could begin work immediately.

However, Savashni continued to use Interview Dynamics to prepare for other job interviews as she was fully committed to the process. This is what she has to say:

"I met with Ossy in January 2014 for a position advertised for a certain company. Unfortunately I did not manage to secure an interview, but the effect of my meeting with Ossy did not end there.

I have since been to various agencies and interviews and, as of last week, I was successful in securing three jobs -- all finance related, at three different companies. That was such a surprise, from having no interviews to securing three jobs. Based on my career path, I chose the first company and will be starting with them in the 2nd week of April.

All of this was possible because I used the tips and advice I received from Ossy. I used his techniques and focused on my key achievements and abilities and put myself forward to each of my interviewers as a business, not just as an individual. His techniques really helped me to build my self-confidence.

My meeting with Ossy was really a life lesson that I shall take with me into my future. I honestly don't believe that I would have been so successful in all three interviews if I did not use Ossy's Interview Dynamic techniques.

Thank you very much. I wish Ossy and the business everything of the best for the future.

Kind Regards,
Savashni"

Should you be interested in obtaining these techniques, log onto **www.jobmasters.co.za**

Change your world. Don't miss out on achieving your career goals due to poor interviewing skills.

Thank you for reading my version of how to prepare for your forthcoming interview. The effort that you put into this concept will improve your chances of taking your business to the next level.

Break Through Your Barriers & Live Your Dreams

SANDRA WESTLAND

Every woman deserves to feel powerful and successful, and the opportunity to do so stands right before her. She doesn't have to be a warrior to smite every dragon or burn down every obstacle that stands in her way. She simply needs to connect with and be her real, authentic self. So her journey to success begins by standing still, by being curious about the world of potential that exists within her and in front of her, and by understanding her inner world in order to ignite change in her outer one towards her success.

But, what stops her from becoming the author of her own life, from being all she can be? The glass ceiling, the unofficial barrier that prevents women from rising up to executive positions or from running their successful businesses, does still exist. Yet, in my twenty-five years of education, hypno-psychotherapy and peak performance training, I see, more significantly, an individual's own inner glass ceiling capping and limiting the success in life that is there for the taking.

To be a woman is to be extraordinary. We all have it within us to move beyond an ordinary life and its everyday limitations to embrace our desires and possibilities, harness our untold natural potential and live the life we are meant to live —a life of personal freedom in which we simply are our natural, awesome selves. Your power is switched on when you embrace, embody, express and enjoy being a woman. Your energy is released when you learn to live truly in your own skin. I love being a woman, and I love continuing to find out just what that is like for me.

This is a journey of discovering your place in life as a woman and as a woman in business, a voyage into your inner mind's processing and the terrain of your inner world, deeper than your conscious mind can be aware of. It is an expedition through self-alignment, forming the detail of your desired outcomes, shaping your life to fit with your passions, sourcing the energy that drives you, thus smashing your glass ceiling and allowing your transformation to unfold. Just as I experienced my own first steps, I want you also to stride out along this path and the journey of becoming your potential. The message I write within the pages of *Smashing Your Glass Ceiling* takes you through this fascinating journey where "Wow, I didn't realize that" and "No wonder I wasn't getting to where I wanted to" are familiar insights.

HOW DOES IT ALL WORK?

The tools you will need for such a journey of self-discovery are drawn from Neuro-Linguistic Programming (NLP), guided imagery, and a gentle questing into uncovering your own uniqueness and meaning in life. In blending these time-tested methods into one programme, it's possible to break through all that's holding you back in life.

From my own personal experience as a woman and as a psychotherapist and trainer, I've found that one of the most powerful tools we naturally have and need to embrace first is the power of imagination; even if you think you have one or not, you really do have an amazing, creative imagination. It just may need awakening and a little encouraging. I would love to show you just how powerful your imagination can be and how crucial it is to connect with you and be your own woman. In beginning this imaginative journey, you are sparking off a chain of events that produce fundamental changes in your physical body, starting with the neurological processes that will link to your biology and produce within you "decision states" leading to the different outcomes that you want, easily and naturally. Imagine the decisions that you can make or the actions that you can take when you are feeling confident, in balance and aligned to your vision, compared to the choices that you opt for when you are upset, anxious, depressed and out of sync with yourself.

By guiding your imagination, you can form an internal vision in which you are taking the right path for you to succeed in your life, and then formulate just what that is. As you immerse yourself in the excitement and the thrill of being on the right road to greatness, you tap into the inner confidence and self-reliance, inner freedom and success awareness that generate your momentum to smashing your glass ceiling. The power is always within you. It's just a case of summoning and connecting with it.

Imagine also gaining new understanding into how you process information from your "now" experiences, how you view the world, how you communicate with others and how they communicate with you. Imagine how much easier your life would be. You can learn how to recognize ways of processing external data and how, by modifying your communication in a way that makes sense to others, your relationships become infinitely warmer, richer and more connected.

Think about meeting me in the flesh for the first time, already knowing how my inner world works. Wouldn't it be good to know I'm an auditory person? Why? Well, my world is very much filtered through sounds. I will be finely tuned into noise ... all noise. I will get distracted with too much of it, and I will recognize very slight changes in your voice, tone and pitch. So I will hear a hint of doubt or an emotion rising from within you just by hearing your voice. If you speak too slowly or very loudly, this will create a dissonance within me. If you use language that talks about "viewing something" or "seeing what you mean" or "having a handle on this or that" instead of "sounds like" or "listen to", I will feel a mismatch between us. Don't click your pen or tap it on the table if you want me to be relaxed! It's only a slight inner discomfort, but it undeniably shapes how I experience you and your communication. Upon our meeting, if you appreciate my world and I appreciate yours, we will hit it off with ease. I will look to communicate to you through your world, which may be visual, auditory, kinesthetic or auditory digital, all very different ways of experiencing and processing, and you can do the same for me.

GETTING TO KNOW YOUR GLASS CEILING

Your internal glass ceiling may have been created from prejudgments, prejudices, cultural and social attitudes that operate deep within the unconscious, taken in when young. So, it's crucial to find these out and know how they work for you, to understand the inner conflicts that are holding you back and what they mean. In speaking with a senior executive upon her reading *Smashing Your Glass Ceiling*, she'd suddenly become aware of how she was dressing like a man for her banking boardroom meetings. It wasn't her at all, but after further exploration, she realized she had unconsciously thought it would help men relate to her and allow her to be "taken seriously". She was shocked at how unconscious this had been, but she was relieved to learn it and is now enjoying the fun of finding out who she is as a woman in business and what clothes this exploration leads her to wearing. It is only by excavating these unconscious gender biases and other judgments that contribute towards making your own ceiling that you can reveal your real, natural self to yourself and the world. In understanding yourself more and knowing just who you are and how you are in the world, you become free to choose how to respond to situations and to people, and then you really begin to own your own life.

I am wondering just what you are thinking, having read these thousand plus words. Is this possible for you or is your glass ceiling giving you bother, preventing you from imagining and thinking of all that you can be? What does your ceiling hold and what is it whispering to you right now? What is your "default" setting?

Are you someone who assumes you won't find a car parking space and prove yourself right, or do you simply know that it doesn't matter where you park and thus usually find one just when and where you need it? Is a potential redundancy at work a chance to do something different, or a terrible catastrophe that you will never escape? Your attitudes play a massive part in your life experiences, and to how much you can grow. Zig Ziglar's famous saying "Your attitude determines your altitude" is so true. So, how do your attitudes determine how successful you can be?

I have lived and refined through my own personal journey a framework of all the things that are crucial to help you aspire to be. Let's make a start right now, something to get you thinking. Let's peek into those achieving just what you want and begin to emulate some of what they do and how they are. It's as good a place as any to start!

In NLP terms, this is called "modeling". In modeling the behaviors and habits of successful people, we're seeking to learn from successful businesswomen and successful women just what it is that they do, and what it is that they have that makes them successful; not to become them, but to incorporate their winning behaviours into our repertoire, choosing those which are congruent with us and amplifying them. I often explore other women that I admire and am drawn to. In carefully watching what they do and exploring this within my own life, in my way, I can open up to further resources that I naturally have, but have yet to connect with. In Sue Knight's' words, "If you spot it, you've got it." (NLP at Work, 2013)

Now to stoke up those neurological pathways as we vamp it up a little more and transport you forward into your own fabulous future. Familiarize yourself with the state of being successful with no glass ceiling, as if you've already accomplished that level of success, a dress rehearsal if you like. Put on the mantle of success and ask yourself how and what do you feel, how would your day evolve, what can you do now that you couldn't do before. How would others perceive you? Get your brain to make it a done deal so that it can look for it, search it out and create it. This is the self-fulfilling prophecy at its most positive, potent and powerful.

Anticipate now becoming friendly and familiar with a future you who has everything you need and want and to be able to use the guidance of that future you – the answers may very well surprise you. My future self enlightened me as to my fear of success! This helped me find my inner glass ceiling and the meaning of it all, so I could smash it and really begin to find out just what I could do and what was possible in life. I believe that to guide others you have to have lived the journey yourself, and so my own personal journey has and is this path too, encompassing where I am finding myself … as a woman, an educator, therapist and businesswoman. This is a journey I don't ever intend to stop.

PEELING BACK THE ONION

There is so much more to explore! As humans, we've infinite depths, so exploring your inner beliefs, your values and mission is crucial for success. It's the peeling back of the onion, layer by layer (corny, I know), but I assure you that the exploration, while deep, is richly rewarding. Wouldn't you rather know what's holding you back and why you may feel frustrated with yourself? I know I would. I simply want to make the most of my time on this earth and experience it as much as possible. Life is to be lived and not simply endured and got through.

Excavate your inner beliefs, isolate the limiting ones that have held you back, and then you will easily and naturally begin to fly! Once figured out, you become empowered as you re-think and re-frame beliefs into being resourceful, productive and desirable, and turn them into second nature.

Let's go one deeper. Do you know just what it is that you value, all those things that are really important to you? Are they aligned with your life? These are your GPS, and if you're frustrated, feel trapped in the mundane of life or have unwanted physical/emotional symptoms, then value fine-tuning is needed for you to move forward in the direction that you want to go. Let's not be sidetracked by detours, road closures and an unclear destination. Being authentic and all that you need to know is what you value so that you're able to craft your mission for the ultimate alignment. In *Smashing Your Glass Ceiling* or my Success workshops , you will not short-change yourself here. I will journey with you, helping you along the way through a process of simple, yet profoundly powerful steps.

When you are fully aligned, there will be no holding you back. You'll meet the right person at the right time, and you'll have the right skills to achieve your goals. Everything will fall into place like a jigsaw puzzle, and you'll have "the strength, the patience, and the passion to reach for the stars", to borrow the words of a courageously inspiring woman, Harriet Tubman.

LOADING UP ON INTERNAL RESOURCES

It's not all plain sailing, and you *will* be derailed by the unexpected, but what makes someone a success is their ability to keep going, even when challenged. So, one of the final steps in the Programme is to load you up with the internal resources to get you through when things get sticky, and when, quite frankly, you wonder why you bother. NLP strategies reprogram how we react and respond to such times, making a monumental difference to how you experience your life. If you're feeling down on yourself, I will show you that you can change your physiology. If you're getting increasingly anxious about an upcoming meeting, you can change your self-talk, the inner conversation you're having with yourself, to something more upbeat, more encouraging and more positive.

Powerful NLP strategies are there for you to use at any time and in any situation. Your life will be richer and filled with more options when you are able to redirect your thinking and focus, stay resourceful in stressful situations, and generate behaviors and outcomes that are positive for you and your life.

Finally, if this chapter has inspired you to delve deeper into Smashing your Glass Ceiling, the book comes with a number of bonuses, some of which can be downloaded from my website, www.SmashingYourGlassCeiling.com for you to enjoy absolutely free. So, get started now and embrace the fact that you are an extraordinary woman.

TAKING THE FIRST STEP

All of us have to start somewhere. I did when I was thirty-four, when I found myself looking at twenty-six more years before retirement, counting the years and the days till the next school holiday. Not how I imagined my life would be.

By becoming curious, asking questions of myself and tapping into effective life-changing techniques that opened me up to the power and potential of the mind, I'm on a fascinating journey. I'm continuing to smash my own internal glass ceiling, and am living out my passion to enhance the lives of other women. I am certainly not "sorted out", nor have I "self-actualized" and not every day is "grrreat", but I know that every day is an adventure with the chance to grow further and find out more about just what is possible.

The more women I meet and work with, the more I learn and the more I gather evidence to support my belief that, as women, we owe it to ourselves to be extraordinary. This is my invitation to you to take the first steps with me on your own journey of becoming all you wish to be.

Sandra Westland is an experienced educator, therapist and successful businesswoman who helps others to find their passion and fulfil their dreams. She has a Master's degree in Existential Psychotherapy, an Education Honours degree, and is a practicing Advanced Hypnotherapist and NLP practitioner. Her doctoral thesis explores women and their relationship with their bodies. She is the author of Smash Your Glass Ceiling and co-author of Thinking Therapeutically.

Sandra is a Director of the Contemporary College of Therapeutic Studies, where she trains people at life changing junctures to be aspiring therapists, so they too can enjoy the enriching privilege of helping others to find their path in life. She is also a co-founder of Self Help School™, which provides psycho-education for the public and is an international speaker on the power of the mind for change.

The Speed of Light

Live and Thrive in the Flow When It Gets Too Much Too Fast

VALERIE KANAY HART

If you want to find the secrets of the universe, think in terms of energy, frequency and vibration.

-Nikola Tesla

LAY DOWN THE LAW

The Law of Vibration tells us that EVERYTHING vibrates in constant motion. That includes the stars overhead, the ground on which we stand and you and I! Our minds tell us that we are solid bodies with a fixed sense of self, but on an energetic level we are changing and shifting all the time. Today, many of us feel that our world is accelerating, spinning on its axis faster and faster. It can feel like too much too fast, but we have to keep the pace in order to avoid being left behind. You have to step up your game and you have to know what to do and when to do it, right? The pivotal question then becomes, with all of life speeded up, how fast do you want to change and how fast can you fully change? If you're serious about transformation, then the answer must be: at the speed of light!

Change at this speed happens effortlessly when you start living your life in the flow. Discover how to slip into the flow in my book The Speed of Light, which will help you create a new vibrant, healthy, and loving relationship with your truth. You must align our mind-body connection to the God of your own understanding, and you can only thrive when you act on every available opportunity to move your lives forward. Visit www.thespeedoflightbook. com to learn why and how your life becomes more meaningful and abundant when you have a worthwhile ambition to pursue.

SHIFTING SIGNALS

Everything is happening faster and faster, and we are the champions of personal evolution. That statement may not describe you right now because you feel stuck in a rut. Maybe you are feeling that you are standing still while the rest of the world is passing you by. If you are, I urge you to commit to breaking the shackles that keep you stuck. When you do, you will begin to experience richer, deeper connections for a more meaningful life. You will also gain the freedom to do what you love, choosing when you want to do it and how you like it to be done. You are a born winner and will succeed. Get the tools you need for success at www.thespeedoflightbook.com.

You know you are stuck when you cannot seem to create change in your life, no matter what you do. To get out of this rut requires becoming aware of the signals you are sending out into your personal vibrational universe. What thoughts are racing through your mind right now? Are they thoughts of complaint and scarcity, of disappointment and regret? Or are they thoughts of hope, optimism and faith because you know the Universe listens and wants to give you everything you desire? The Law of Attraction tells us that your thoughts and feelings communicate your desires to the universe, which then mirrors those requests back to you. However, it is important to realize that today's predicament is not tomorrow's future.

Yes, your reality reflects an order that you placed directly with the universe, however unconsciously. No matter how your life looks now, I know you have the power to change it because you can become more conscious, and this is the solution to everything. When you raise your level of consciousness, you come into direct energetic alignment with the energies that shape galaxies and universes and you achieve a wholesome, satisfying and fulfilled life. Just as importantly, you don't have to wait years for these changes to manifest; the secret is that they can happen immediately. In less time than it takes for your heart to thump its beat, you can change your world and your reality.

What change would you like to see first? Is it to create a better balance between work and family? Is it to get out of your comfort zone by expanding your boundaries to unknown and untried territories? Is it to align with your purpose and to positively impact the world? Share your vision at www. thespeedoflightbook.com.

WAKE AND SHAKE UP YOUR DREAMER

Not all those who wander are lost. – J.R.R Tolkien

My grandmother raised me from the time I was 3 months old, and growing up, I often traveled with her to visit her father, who lived in Sylvester, Georgia. We always travelled by bus, and she would take the aisle seat so I could look out the window and dream. Instead of seeing the cotton fields and roadside junk as we drove by, all I saw was the two of us on a giant airplane, flying to fun and exciting places. The roar of the bus became the roar of Niagara Falls, and I saw myself hiking up Mt. Kilimanjaro or even sledding down the Himalayas. If we got talking with other passengers, I always told them I was born and raised in San Francisco because of the Golden Gate Bridge!

After we arrived at my great-grandfather's house and I told him of our adventures, he'd always say 'oh, you are dreamer' and I'd say, 'yes I am!' That simple bus trip was the beginning of my love of travel – throughout my life I've always moved around at a moment's notice, even when I don't know what awaits me in my new home. Great-Grandpa always played along with my long-winded stories of how I'd come to see him this time, so he would always ask how my flight was, and what other adventures I'd had on my way. I'd say we went over the bridge to have lunch with our friends and then climbed the mountains during the 10-minute layover we'd had in Cairo, GA, or some other fanciful tale!

This lifelong love of adventure has driven me to live in places as diverse as New York, Los Angeles and the rainforests of Costa Rica. What are your dreams? What do you want that you do not currently have? Are you secretly envious of those who've quit their jobs in order to travel around the world? Do you wish to write a book? Open a pet store? Be a public speaker?

I call on you to dust off those dreams that lie dormant and unrealized after years of neglect. You are entitled to live the life that only you can dream of; in fact, it's your birthright to live the life of your dreams. Start by speaking about those precious hopes and dreams; giving voice to them is your first step towards making them real. Start by telling me tell me at www.thespeedoflightbook.com. I promise you your dreams will be treated with as much delicate care as the precious jewels they truly are.

TO GET WHAT YOU WANT, MAKE YOUR OWN LUCK

Luck favors the prepared mind. – Louis Pasteur

As you gain clarity and laser-like focus, you will begin to operate in the zone and your life will flow like magic. You will find yourself more and more in the right place at the right time, forging connections with people who have the resources to help you get what you want. It will feel like magic because it will be effortless and it will be easy. The synchronicities will become like beautiful butterflies that show up everywhere, when you learn to thrive in this way.

To be in the flow, you only need to relax and allow. A relaxed mind creates space that allows good things to happen, knowing there is plenty to go around for everyone. You can only put something into a hand that is opened, and thus able to receive, open up to receive what is available to you right now. It is no accident that you are reading this book at this time; I wrote it for you, knowing it would find you when time was right. And the right time for you is now, this very moment. This is the moment when you make the positive and deliberate changes that will impact the rest of your life.

There is abundant evidence of synchronicities that you can see every day. Some chalk it up to luck, but while luck may play a role, a bit of preparation on your part doesn't hurt. It's true that opportunities are always coming your way, but you can only take advantage of them if you are sufficiently prepared. Ask yourself what you need to do to prepare to live your dreams, and then make those things your first priority.

HARNESSING YOUR INTUITIVE MIND

The intuitive mind is a sacred gift, and the rational mind is a faithful servant. We have created a society that honors the servant and has forgotten the gift. - Albert Einstein

We waste so much precious time and energy trying to figure everything out with our rational minds, but the intuitive mind and the mind of God are one and the same. This mind is within all of us, and it has all the answers, if we can just relax and let them emerge. Only God can see the big picture, but we can allow that picture to unfold through our relationship with the God of our own understanding.

Just a glimpse of the big picture is all you need to get the juices flowing. Do not worry about how your vision will unfold, let God be the architect and trust that He will orchestrate outcomes that defy your highest expectations. Keep the faith and keep open - the details will be given as long as you keep your spiritual ear to the ground and follow all the signs you receive.

Intuition is a powerful and miraculous ability to know something and not know why you know it, without any rational proof. You must choose to trust where it leads you, without understanding why.

I like to travel and have fun, so one evening recently I went to the Silver Star Casino in Philadelphia, to try my luck so to speak. On that particular night no one in the gaming section was doing well, and the atmosphere was extremely intense. Personally, I only engage in games of chance when I get that knowing feeling. In that intense atmosphere I just asked myself a simple, silent question: how would I know which slot machine would give me $1000? I don't know where that thought came from or why, but I knew not to ignore this hunch.

I knew that lady luck did not seem to be in the house that night, but my focus didn't waver as I inserted the money and immediately locked the first winning blue, then the second one, and the final jackpot-winning diamond. I had won $1600 with no effort, just by allowing the mind of God to work through me. I couldn't stop laughing and, without reservations, yelled THANK YOU! THANK YOU! I LOVE YOU! I knew I had been rewarded for listening to and trusting the voice of my intuition once again. Eventhough the outer environment was "unfriendly", I relied on my inner compass and it pointed me to the right way.

SOUL HAPPY

Laughter is food for the soul and adds vibrancy to our lives. That's why I always tell my clients to stay light-hearted and not take everything, especially themselves, too seriously. When you learn to find the hidden humor in life, you allow the good vibrations to flow throughout your body. The happier you are, the better you feel, and the deeper your connection will be to your soul.

This link to your soul is so important, because it helps to keeps the rhythm of your life upbeat and promotes a positive attitude, good health, and peak performance. Along with laughing hard and often, think happy and positive thoughts and create a beautiful clutter-free environment for yourself so you can think straight. In the same way that our inner thoughts create our outer reality, the outer space does have an impact on our inner orientation. Which would you naturally prefer? A crowded room filled with unwanted junk or a peaceful zen-like room for meditation? For most of you, I am sure it's the latter because you have room to just breathe and just be.

I cannot overplay the importance of just being. Ever morning, I stay still for a few minutes at the start of each day, to simply contemplate how I will spend your time on this earth in a meaningful way. It's a beautiful practice and while it seems we are doing and achieving nothing, think on this. It's ironic but true that when you take this time, you make more time, because you gain clarity on those priorities that most significantly impact your dreams.

What is the big change your soul deeply and fervently desires to see? If you don't know immediately what it is, give yourself the richness of a few minutes in quiet and solitude and the start of every day. Pretty soon, answers will bubble up from your inner most consciousness. I would love to hear about these whisperings from your soul at www.thespeedoflightbook.com.

THE MEANING OF CHOICE

If you really want to change your life, you must stop doing things that harm you and replace them with expressions of self-love. What do I mean by harmful things? I refer to attitudes like:

- self-deprivation (because you don't deserve more)

- uncalled for sacrifice (because it's expected of you)

- fearing to break out of your limitations (because it's downright scary and who will pick you up when you fall?)

It takes awareness and a conscious decision to shed those harmful habits and attitudes. Understand that it's a step-by-step process, and anyone who really wants to change for the better can do so because there is a wealth of resources available to all of us.

There is a vast amount of information available from the media and internet, and in conversations, books, courses and so forth. With so many resources, how do you choose which to pursue? I prefer the simplest and most effective approach, which is to pursue what resonates with your heart and your intentions for your life. There is nothing greater in life than living from your soul's purpose and passion. I offer a fuss-free, simple method; find out more http://www.thespeedoflightbook.com

With the right tools and intentions, you will be able to enter a higher realm where it will be impossible to return to old ways that no longer serve you. From this place, you will be using your God-given talents, strengths and passions to be totally present in your life, and you will become a beacon to your family, friends, loved ones and the community.

THE DIFFERENCE

In order to live in the flow, we have to clear out mental negativity. Every problem has a solution and the solution always lies in transcending the thinking that caused the problem. If you study people who are living out their dreams, you'll discover that they had to overcome many obstacles, some seemingly surmountable. No human being gets to escape troubles; the key is to realize that you are bigger than any problem and believing in your own strength and potential to find a way around the bumps on the road.

Here are some key characteristics that these heroes tend to share:

- they have skillfully mastered problem-solving in order to get what they want

- they make good decisions;

- they do what's required to get the results they want.

Very often, they establish working relationships with like-minded people and get assistance from others. Successful people know that life is a team sport. They strategically choose to surround themselves with smart people who help them focus on what's right instead of dwelling on what's wrong. Leveraging the energy and resources of a group turbo-charges such smart people towards their goals. You too can travel at warp speed towards your goals. Learn more on how to build the beneficial connections that fast-forward you to your deepest desires and most treasured goals at www.thespeedoflightbook.com.

HARMONY IS SWEET

Harmony is sweet and good for you in every way, just like honey is. Remember that life is one indivisible whole, not just the fragments of your past, present, and future. In recognition of this, be careful to look neither too far back nor too far ahead. When you center your attention on the present moment, you bring all your power to it, and everything works because everything is connected right now.

When the atmosphere is harmonious, it operates free of the negativity that can put a damper on the flow of positive vibrations. Nurture a healthy love of life and honor yourself and the life you have chosen. Fall in love with your life, with where you are now and what you have at this moment. It may not be everything you desire, but when you are in harmony, life becomes much easier. It is very simple - when you are balanced and centered, you attract and manifest that which you desire very quickly.

Stay in a state of admiration and awe of all blessings that are showered on you, be they large or small. Gratitude attracts more of the same, and keeps you in a state of grace. Celebrate your successes, because the attitude of gratitude and appreciation amps up your drive to perform at peak levels to achieve peak results. Everything has its place, and for harmony to exist we must cultivate a pleasant and positive outlook on everything we encounter. Learn more at www.thespeedoflightbook.com

JUST LIKE THE FLOWERS BLOSSOM

Just like flowers, all of us bloom in unique ways at various stages of our lives. You can't compare yourself with anybody else, because they may just be at a different stage than you are. For example, some babies walk at 9 months, 12 months or even 2 years, but they all walk at some point if they are healthy. Honor the uniqueness of who you are, blossoming and coming full-circle like a flower in bloom.

Be mindful and observe yourself as you are thinking, speaking, and acting. If you can begin to catch yourself falling into old patterns and make corrections in the moment, that will go a long way to ensuring that you will bloom into a radiant flower you were meant to be. Oprah Winfrey says, "Breathe. Let go. And remind yourself that this very moment is the only one you know you have for sure."

We are all at different stages of development, and each is equally beautiful in the eyes of God. Learn more at www.thespeedoflightbook.com.

PEOPLE WHO MAKE IT HAPPEN

What will you do with this one and only life you've been given? How can you make your life a blessing to hundreds, or even millions of people? Our legacy is shaped by how we live each day of our lives, and each decision you make. It is one thing to go through the motions of living, and quite another to live a truly extraordinary and meaningful life that fills you with pure joy and soaring exultation.

I encourage you to share that which you have kept sealed and tucked away, and step into your highest ambitions, no matter how impossible they may seem. It is the work of an Authority to help you achieve your dreams, because we see things differently than you do at this moment. Go to www.thespeedoflightbook.com to learn more.

YOUR POSITIVE LEGACY

The fragrance always remains in the hand that gives the rose. – Heda Bejar

Everything you think, do, or say becomes your legacy. There are no guarantees in life, so make sure you are leaving the impression you want to leave on this world each and every day. What meaning will you make of this marvelous life, and what impact will your message have for others?

Maybe you want a life of more leisure, increased income, a new career or you're an entrepreneur seeking more business. If you're a student, maybe you want better grades, or maybe have no idea what you want of life yet. No matter where you are in life, know that nothing is impossible. You have the questions, and the Authority has the answers. Learn more at www. thespeedoflightbook.com.

As an Authority in the field of personal evolution, I can help you to achieve this life by deliberate design. Raise the bar on your personal evolution so you can see results faster than you ever could have imagined or thought possible. Learn to follow your intuition, so you can live your life in the flow and experience a whirlwind of synchronicities that will uplift you into new world beyond your wildest dreams. I invite you to transform in twinkling of an eye, at the speed of light.

Family is
Everything

DAN ROGERS

Hundreds of years ago wooden ships brought immigrants to the shores of what would become the maritime provinces of Canada. Why did the pioneers brave starvation, malnutrition, disease or shipwreck?

Today, a number of immigrants arrived at Pearson International Airport in Toronto, Ontario. Why did they leave their countries, their jobs and friends to try and carve out a new life in Canada?

Ask such questions of either group and you would likely receive the identical answer: "To build a better life for my family," they would say. Why? Because family is everything!

In 1916 a young couple, Clarence and Lizzy, got married and boarded a train to northwest Saskatchewan. The rules were that if you were over eighteen, married and agreed to live on and work the land, the government would grant you a quarter section, which is 160 acres or 65 hectares.

At first they plowed the virgin fields with a team of oxen. The prairie grass roots were so thick that the girl had to follow along behind the plow, cutting the roots of the prairie grass with a butcher knife. Her first three babies miscarried. Then, on her fourth pregnancy, the boy rounded up just enough money for one train ticket to the closest town that had a hospital (Lloydminster). He took her in a horse drawn wagon across the prairie for many kilometers to the train station, put her on the train and returned home to continue working the fields. The girl gave birth to a healthy baby girl named Grace. That baby girl was my mother.

My grandmother was what was known as a Bernardo child. She was in a program based out of England that was founded by a man named Bernardo. Orphans and children whose parents could not afford to look after them were shipped to Canada to live on farms. Some of the families treated the child as one of their own, while others treated the child as a slave. The end result, however, was that they got to Canada. And it worked, albeit slowly. So … my mother had a better life than her mother … I am having a better life than my mother … and my son, an only child, came home from the hospital not only to his own bedroom, but to one that had a four piece en suite bathroom. Also, by the time my wife and I are gone from this world, he will be an automatic millionaire.

My hope is that you and your family can accomplish this quicker than we did. We were slow learners. It took us over a century to create wealth. But the fact that you are in Canada and reading this book already puts you in the group that is most likely to succeed. Do you find that hard to believe? Then just think of all the people who came home from work today and are either checking Facebook or watching reality TV. They definitely aren't reading a book about how to succeed financially.

THE PURPOSE OF THIS CHAPTER

The purpose of this chapter is to help educate you to use whatever money you have to benefit you and your family in the long run.

The first thing I want to do is ask you a question: What is your biggest asset? Many people will answer that question by stating what they own. Various answers will be the most obvious ones like my house, my car, my life insurance policy, my retirement fund. But the real answer is you or, to be more accurate, it's your ability to earn a living.

Now, consider that the average annual income in Canada is around fifty thousand dollars (at time of printing). That means in a typical forty year career you will have grossed two million dollars. Yet, most Canadians don't own two million dollars of mortgage free real estate or don't have two million dollars in the bank or even in an insurance policy. Why is that?

It's simple mathematics …

Mr. A and Mr. B both moved to Canada about fifty years ago from the same country. They both got jobs at the same company for the same wage. But Mr. A saved up his money for a down payment on a house and also budgeted in the monthly premium for a permanent life insurance policy, while Mr. B spent much of his disposable income on trips back to his homeland, coffee shops, take- out food, and cigarettes.

Both A and B died about twenty years ago. The daughter of Mr. A inherited a mortgage free house and a life insurance policy, while the son of Mr. B ended up with nothing. Because the child of A immediately had cash in hand, from the insurance money, and she chose to live in the house for free, she was able to invest both the life insurance money and the monthly rent she had previously been paying. Meanwhile, the son of Mr. B had to save for years and years before he could get out of the apartment he was renting, because saving up while paying rent is much more challenging. In the end, however, B descendent was able to buy a house and make some modest investments.

Eventually the heirs of both Mr. A and Mr. B died. The grandchildren of A have inherited multiple real estate properties and investment funds easily worth in excess of a million dollars, while the family of Mr. B ended up with only a few hundred thousand, as the real estate and other investments were purchased later in their parents' lives and didn't have time enough to grow. The property may not have even been mortgage free at the time of Mr. B's death.

So, the third generation of the A family are now millionaires, while the same generation of the B family has enough money for a modest down payment on a nice house.

You want to be Mr or Mrs A. Buy a home early and pay off that mortgage. Protect your ability to earn with the proper insurance policies and invest on an ongoing basis. Read on, I'll show you how to do it. But first a discussion about estate planning

WILL AND POWER OF ATTORNEY

We have been talking about estates. These are passed on to beneficiaries through the vehicle known as the will. But, over the several years that I have been in this profession, I have encountered a rather high percentage of people that do not have their wills done. And you do need one. Not a "do it yourself" will kit that can be purchased online or at a business supply retailer. Generally, the legal system does not consider this type of will to be valid. No, I strongly urge you to have a lawyer draw up your will. A good lawyer. A conscientious lawyer. Here's why …

An elderly widower sells his house, puts the money in the bank, moves to an apartment, and marries a much younger new wife. His lawyer draws up a will stating that his estate will be divided amongst his wife, his three children and his two favourite charities. The lawyer did not enquire about what type of account the money was in or ask any questions of that nature. When the man died, the executor of the estate found out that the bank had advised the man to name a beneficiary to the account, so the man, not being given a full legal explanation of the ramifications, named his wife as beneficiary. So, on his death, the bank immediately transferred 100% of the funds into the wife's name, and there was no legal recourse to get her to divide up the money according to the will. The will became a useless piece of paper. The three children and the two charities received nothing from the fund. That man was my father.

The lesson to be learned is to never assume that a professional you hire is automatically going to do things in your best interest.

Power of Attorney: There are two types of power of attorney: one for personal care, and one for property. This means that you designate a person to make decisions on your behalf should you reach the point where you can no longer make these decisions yourself. **Personal care** refers to topics such as choosing a personal support worker, a nursing home, treatments, medications, and other things of that nature. **Property** refers to topics such as whether or not to sell the house or rent it out or authorize repairs, and whether to sell the car, or cut the lawn or many other property related items.

In listing a power of attorney, remember that you do not have to have the same person for all areas. You could have a daughter who would be the best for personal care, an eldest son who would make the best executor, and a youngest son who is in real estate who would be the best person for property decisions.

I should also mention **Probate** as it is a complicated and frequently costly procedure wherein you must prove the validity of the will. The general rule is that if there is a beneficiary listed on the account, then probate is not required.

When the funds are in a bank, the money could be in one of several different types of accounts. It could be in a chequing account, a savings account, a TFSA (tax free savings account), an RRSP (registered retirement savings plan), mutual funds, segregated funds, GIC (guaranteed investment certificate), a RIF (retirement income fund), and a number of others. The bank would likely ask you to name a beneficiary on the account. This is done to prevent probate. However, remember the story about my father and learn from it. If there is only one person that you want to give your money to, then that is fine, but if there are multiple people, you must name them all.

PROTECT YOURSELF

In order to open this discussion, we need to go back to the reason everyone comes to Canada in the first place. We all know the answer to that one: to build a better life for your family. At the same time, we need to recall your greatest asset. It's you, and if you go down, everything that you worked for could be lost. So we are going to address a very important issue, income replacement. This is generally broken down into two areas; disability coverage and critical illness coverage.

Disability coverage: Disability insurance is meant to replace part of your income (usually 55%) in case of injury or illness. Now, the first thing to know is that not all disability policies are equal. Some give you the right see your own doctor—some do not. And that makes all the difference. The first group of claimants tends to be entrepreneurs who don't want to be away from their jobs any longer than the insurance company wants them to be. The second group of claimants tends to be more the corporate type, a type that encompasses malingerers—those people who are in no rush to get back to work after an injury or illness—the type that breeds distrust in the insurance companies. Make sure you're in the first group.

Integration of benefits: What this means is that if you signed up for a $2,000/month disability policy and you get hurt, and another organization also agrees to pay you let's say $1,200/month, whether it is another insurance company, Workers Safety Insurance Board, the employer, or whomever, then your insurance company only has to pay you the difference of $800/month. You can find policies that don't have this clause.

Return of Premium: What if you are lucky and never get injured? How would you like to get all your money back when you retire, tax free? Yes, there are disability policies available that have this benefit.

Soft tissue injuries/back injuries/sprains/strains: This is another very important feature. Many disability providers are so concerned about people faking injuries that they won't pay out unless something shows up on an X-ray. You don't want a policy like that. You want a policy that will cover you in all cases of injury or illness.

Injury occurs on or off the job: Many employers who provide a benefit plan to their employees will have disability coverage that only covers on the job accidents. While better than nothing, statistically, the average Canadian is more likely to get hurt in a car accident, at home, or while participating in sports and leisure than actually getting hurt on the job. That' the kind of coverage you want.

No limit on number of claims made: This one is fairly self-explanatory.

Make sure your provider does not have a clause where they can terminate your coverage if you make too many claims.

Critical Illness/Hospital Sickness Benefits: Let's imagine that you or your spouse were diagnosed with a terminal illness or a debilitating disease. The ill person might wish to do their "bucket list," go back to visit the homeland, see the Seven Wonders of the World, or take a cruise around the world. But from where would the money come? Cash in RRSPs? Sell the house? Remortgage the house? The problem with doing that is it ruins the whole game plan of coming to Canada to build a better life for your children and your children's children.

This is the reason that critical illness coverage exists in a place that already has state funded health care.

And just like disability coverage, it is possible to get critical illness coverage with a Return of Premium Clause, meaning that if you remain in good health, you get your money back at the end.

LIFE INSURANCE

There are many different types of life insurance. It is vitally important for you to know the differences so that you can pick the type that is the right one for your situation.

Reason for life insurance: Do you have massive debt from a mortgage or business loan that if all goes well you will have paid off before retirement? Or do you want to leave your family a lump sum of money for a particular purpose, regardless of whether you die young or old? These two situations require (differing) insurance products.

The standard formula that the insurance industry uses for determining the amount of coverage is: ten times annual salary plus debt. So if you make the average Canadian income of about $50,000 per year and have a three hundred thousand dollar mortgage, then the calculation would be to have $800,000 in coverage.

Term Insurance: Term insurance would be better understood by the public if it were renamed "temporary insurance." With term insurance you are buying a window of time. If you die in that window of time, the insurance company writes a cheque to your beneficiary. If you die outside that window, they cut no cheque at all.

Permanent insurance: Permanent insurance is frequently known by its official name, whole life insurance. If the reason for buying is that you need some security to pay off your debts if you die young, then term is the way to go, but if you want to leave a lump sum to your family whether you die next year or in sixty years, then you will want a permanent product.

Term to 100: Term to 100 is a rather unique type of life insurance that is sort of a hybrid between term insurance and permanent insurance. As we have already read, the disadvantage of a term policy is that it eventually runs out, but the advantage is lower premiums. The disadvantage of whole life coverage is that the premiums are high, but the advantage is that it lasts forever. What if you could get a policy that never runs out but that has the lower premiums more associated with term insurance? Great, right? That's why many companies don't offer the product. But you can find it, if that is what you want.

No Medical Insurance: No medical insurance is frequently called other names such as final expense insurance, funeral insurance, burial insurance, guaranteed issue insurance, instant issue insurance, and perhaps a few other names. It is frequently advertised by way of television commercials, and mail flyers delivered by the post office. The target client is often a retiree whose term insurance has now expired but who still wants to leave a lump sum when he or she dies. People with health problems who will never qualify for standard application coverage also tend to buy this type of policy.

Universal Life: This is another type of whole life policy. It can be a bit complicated, so I'm going to give a brief explanation of this product here. With a universal life policy, a portion of your premium goes into an investment. Over the years, the idea is for the investment to grow substantially. A universal life policy with a face amount of $100,000 would have an additional investment portion attached to it, so after a few decades the policy might pay out in total $150,000, $200,000 or more. Although this seems like a great idea, low interest rates over the past several years have made many people who hold a universal life policy realize that the projected payout at the end is going to be considerably lower than what the agent had suggested way back when the policy was first taken out.

The moral of this story is to make sure you sit down with a financial professional who will do a "needs analysis."

PLANNING FOR RETIREMENT

RRSP stands for Registered Retirement Savings Plan. An RRSP isn't an investment, it's a shell in which you can store all sorts of different kinds of financial plans and investments.

An RRSP could contain stocks, bonds, mutual funds, segregated funds, Guaranteed Investment Certificates, syndicate mortgages, Guaranteed Investment Accounts, just to name some of the more popular products that a typical Canadian RRSP might contain.

What an RRSP does is let you defer income tax. It is designed for Canadians who know that they are going to be bringing in less money after they retire than they are currently bringing in now. Canada Revenue Agency (CRA) charges income tax on a sliding scale depending on the income of the person. Someone who doesn't earn much income may pay no income tax at all, where someone with a high income might pay out 40% of their pay to income tax.

Life Income Fund: A life income fund generally comes from a company pension. Some employers offer a company matched retirement plan, meaning that whatever you put into it, they will contribute an equal amount. When you leave the company, it is recommended that you do something with it. The reason is that if the company runs into financial trouble, your retirement fund could be gone, or at least reduced. It has happened before, and will most likely happen again. Instead, if you quit, get downsized, or retire, you should move that money out of there and put it with an investment firm. That way, the success of your former employer will have no influence on the fund.

Various investments

Mutual funds are what are known as securities. The agent or broker must hold a license regulated by each provinces securities commission. Mutual funds are really just a collection of various stocks. They were designed for the purpose of the small investor being able to get into the stock market without a large cash outlay and with a lower risk. There are thousands of different funds out there, and virtually all of them are quite heavily diversified. This is both good news and bad news. The good news is that if one or a few of the companies that are inside that particular mutual fund take a huge nose dive, it won't cause your fund to drop too dramatically. The bad news is really the opposite side of the same coin. If a few of the stocks in the fund soar tremendously, your fund won't go up all that much because of all the other stocks in there that remain steadfast or have dropped. Mutual funds have no guarantees whatsoever, so if your fund dropped way down, you have only two choices: you can cash out at a loss, or you can hold onto it for enough years and hope that it rebounds satisfactorily. Mutual funds are also subject to fees known as Management Expense Ratios, or MER. If your fund's MER is 2%, then on a one hundred thousand dollar investment, expect to pay two thousand dollars per year in fees.

Segregated funds are very similar in concept to mutual funds. Segregated funds are sold by life insurance companies. Many financial experts describe segregated funds as "mutual funds with an insurance policy wrapper". Segregated funds must be kept separate from the insurance company's regular finances, hence the name. A "seg" fund and a mutual fund may both be investing in the same stocks, the main difference between the two, is there is a guarantee with a seg fund. The guarantee in a seg fund is generally either 75% or 100% of the original investment, depending on which plan you take. That means that you are guaranteed to get back either 75% or 100% of your money, even if the fund loses money. You will have to hold onto the fund for an agreed upon length of time, usually ten years to get this guarantee. And it is important to know that this guarantee is not free. A seg fund will have extra fees associated with it to cover this guarantee. If you cash out before the agreed upon time, you get what is in the fund, whether it has gained money or lost money, less any fees. If the seg fund rises in value, most plans will allow you to "reset" the guaranteed amount to this higher amount, however, that would mean that doing this will reset the amount of time, usually ten years, that you must hold the fund.

Depending on which plan you take, 75% or 100%, if you die while the funds are down, your beneficiary will receive 75% or 100% of the fund.

Guaranteed Investment Certificate (GIC): A GIC is a savings account where the interest rate is pre-set. There is an amount of time, generally two years, three years, four years, or five years that you must keep the money in the account in order to obtain that interest rate. If you withdraw the funds earlier than that date, you won't get the agreed upon interest rate. The longer you keep the money locked up, the higher the interest rate you can get.

Guaranteed Investment Account (GIA): The simplest way to describe a GIA is that it is like a GIC, except it is carried by insurance companies, just like seg funds, and the guarantee activates in the event of the contract holder's death.

If the contract holder dies while having a GIA, the company guarantees the highest of the two following things: either the balance of the account on the date of death; or 100% of the sum invested in this account.

Syndicated Mortgages: A developer who wants to build a condo tower, a commercial office building, or any other large construction project can generally only get conventional bank financing up to a certain percentage of the cost of the project. The remainder of the amount he needs has to come from someplace else. When you agree to give the developer your money, you go on title, the same way that your bank is on title for your house, if you have a mortgage. Syndicated mortgages have been around for a long time, but ordinary folk like you and me have only started hearing about them in the past few years. The reason is that they used to be reserved for those with very large sums to invest, like a million dollars. It was only relatively recently that the industry opened up the market dramatically by lowering the minimum investment to twenty five thousand dollars. Generally, the syndicate mortgages that have come across my desk pay 8% per annum, simple interest. It is important to know the difference between simple interest and compound interest. With compound interest, you receive interest on your interest, but with simple interest you do not. A typical syndicate mortgage locks your money away for a period of time, frequently three or four years.

Gold and other precious metals: The only reason that I am even mentioning this topic is because I am told that there are people on the radio urging us to buy gold. On the financial security pyramid or pillars, or ladder, or however you would like to refer to it, precious metals are to be considered at the top, right up there with collecting works of art. This means that it is something that would be recommended to do after your house is mortgage free, and you have amassed considerable wealth and assets.

REAL ESTATE

Buy vs Rent: There are always those who debate whether or not it is better to rent and invest more in the market, or buy real estate, and subsequently have less money left over at the end of the month to invest. Remember that home ownership has two entirely separate goals. The first one is to make money on it, either by buying low and selling high, or by making improvements to the property, thus increasing its value, or by paying off the mortgage so that you no longer have the expense of making payments. The second goal is to improve your quality of life. You have your very own residence without being at the mercy of a landlord, should they decide to sell the property, or raise the rent, or move into it themselves, or move a relative into it. You also have total control over what colour you would like the walls painted, the types of light fixtures, window coverings, faucets, countertops, and a host of other features.

Buying Real Estate: The first thing you will require is the **minimum down payment**. When you buy with less than twenty percent down, this is what the banks refer to as a high ratio mortgage. This requires you to have mortgage default insurance. The most popular organization the banks use to obtain mortgage default insurance is the Canada Mortgage and Housing Corporation (CMHC), a crown corporation. Two other companies that offer this are Genworth Financial Canada, and Canada Guaranty. They will charge a fee, and blend it into your payment. This can only be avoided by having a minimum of twenty percent of the purchase price of the property already saved up and available. For a first time home buyer, this could be difficult. Most of the property purchases I have made had CMHC on them. I still found this to be the lesser of the evils when compared to paying rent.

Next, you will need to **obtain approval for the mortgage**. You should do this before looking at any properties. There are two ways of doing this. The first is to talk to your own bank branch. The second is to use a mortgage broker. The advantage of using a mortgage broker is twofold. First, they do all the work, don't charge you and get paid a referral fee from the financial institution where the mortgage is placed. The second advantage is that they will frequently work with multiple lenders, giving them and you more choices. One thing they will be looking for is your Total Debt Service Ratio (TDSR). This means that all your payments, mortgage, utilities, and other things such as car loan payments and line of credit payments should not exceed approximately forty percent of your overall gross household income. So first of all, you should not be considering real estate if you owe any money on anything else, and yes, that includes your car.

The next thing is your need to have established a **credit rating**. There are two credit rating services. The most popular one is Equifax, and the other one is TransUnion. You can obtain your credit score from these institutions yourself at no charge. They will probably try to get you to pay for it, and they will quite likely offer you the information instantly if you pay, but you can wait and get it the slow way without having to pay. If you are new to the country, or young, or both, you may not have established a credit rating. The first thing is to have a credit card. Obviously, the intended goal is to pay the balance off every statement, thus avoiding any interest payments. If you think you can get by in this world without a credit card, you thought wrong. Not only is it vital in establishing a credit rating, but without one, it is generally quite difficult to purchase anything online, obtain tickets for a major event, rent a car, book a flight, stay in a hotel, and a host of various other situations that will cross your path from time to time.

Types of properties: There are really only four: condo, townhouse, semi, and detached

Condo is short for condominium. You will usually see them in the form of high rise buildings, but there are townhouse condos and even detached condos. With a condo you only own the inside, the condo corporation owns the outside. I'm using simple terminology here. You pay a monthly fee to them and they are responsible for exterior things like the roof, landscaping, snow removal, elevators, and really everything this is not inside your unit.

The next type of property on the scale is the **townhouse**. They can be condos or freehold. If it is a townhouse condo, you pay a fee to the condo corporation, just like a high rise, and they look after the same things like the roof, snow removal, and grass cutting. If it is a freehold, you own the whole thing, and you are responsible for everything. The main items to think about with a townhouse is that you share your walls with someone else.

Next on the list is the **semi-detached**. This has all the same possible downsides as a townhouse, but you are only sharing one wall. The key to a good semi is to have a great neighbour on the other side of the wall. But of course, you have very little way of finding that out until you are already moved in.

A **detached house**, meaning that it is not connected to any other building (you can walk all the way around all four sides), is the ultimate goal, in my humble opinion. In many regions, especially in the Greater Toronto Area (GTA), the detached house is sought after not only for the buffer zone between neighbours, but because many of these houses are ideally suited to having a separate basement apartment with a separate entrance, frequently a side door. This is an excellent way to bring in extra money to offset the high mortgage payment.

GOVERNMENT RETIREMENT BENEFITS

There are five main areas about which you will need to know: Canada Pension Plan (CPP), Canada Pension Plan Survivor Benefit, Canada Pension Plan Death Benefit, Old Age Security (OAS) and Guaranteed Income Supplement (GIS).

The Canada Pension Plan (CPP) is something that you would have paid into during the course of your working career. You can apply for it as early as age sixty or as late as age seventy. If you apply for it at age sixty, you will, however, receive a 36% reduction in benefits. If you apply for it at age seventy, you will get an increase of 42%.

According to the government of Canada statistics as of the year 2015, the average CPP monthly benefit is $619 and the maximum is $1,065.

Old Age Security: The Old Age Security (OAS) is a benefit for which you can apply at age sixty five, as of now, however, there are plans to increase the age at which you can apply to age sixty seven. Time will tell if the federal government sticks to the plan of age sixty seven, or if successive governments decide to roll it back to age sixty five. At time of publishing, the OAS is around $565 per month, however, it is indexed to inflation, so it generally goes up a few dollars per month every year.

CPP Survivor Benefit: If you are the first to die in a spousal or common-law relationship, the surviving spouse should apply for this benefit. It is generally 60% of the deceased partner's monthly CPP benefit, or if death occurs before age sixty five, then this benefit is calculated on the amount that it would have been if death had occurred at age sixty five.

CPP Death Benefit: Only a very few countries offer this benefit. To be eligible for your estate to receive this benefit you must have made contributions to CPP in the lesser of: one third of the calendar years in your CPP contributory period, but no less than three calendar years; or ten calendar years.

The amount of the death benefit depends on how much and for how long the deceased contributed to the CPP. The maximum benefit is $2,500. According to the latest statistics, the average benefit is around $2,300. The CPP death benefit is calculated as the amount equal to six months' worth of your monthly CPP benefit.

Guaranteed Income Supplement (GIS): If you live in Canada and have a low income, this monthly non-taxable benefit can be added to your Old Age Security (OAS) pension, if your annual income (or in case of a couple, your combined income) is less than the maximum annual income. The Canadian government calculates this maximum annual income amount based on numerous different criteria such as if you are single, widowed, or divorced, or if you have a spouse that receives the full OAS pension, or if your spouse does not receive the OAS, or if your spouse is already receiving the GIS and the OAS. You can always go the government's website yourself when you need this information: www.servicecanada.gc.ca

FINAL ARRANGEMENTS

This section will be dealing with an area that most people are not particularly thrilled about discussing. Furthermore, most people are not willing to walk into a funeral home and ask questions. Fortunately, I worked in the industry for ten years, so I'm in the position to not only help you spare your family a lot of grief and hardship, but at the same time, save you money as well.

There are two ways to pre-arrange your funeral: One way is to pre-arrange but not pre-pay. The other, and more preferred way, is to pre-arrange and pre-pay.

Cremation verses Burial: The main reason that 90 % of the people I have talked to about funerals over the years choose cremation, is so they can avoid the cemetery completely.

If you choose cremation, there are five options open to you regarding the disposition of the remains.

1. Your family can take the urn home with them and put it on the shelf. (This is not for everyone, some like the idea, some hate it.)

2. You can have the ashes scattered. Note: this choice is completely legal.

3. If you have an immediate family member that is already in a cemetery plot, most cemetery boards will allow you to place your urn in your family member's plot, generally for a fee of a few hundred dollars.

4. You can purchase your very own plot and have your urn buried there.

5. Cemeteries have structures called columbariums, or wall niches, that you can purchase for the purpose of having your urn placed there permanently.

Funeral Service Choices: For the sake of simplicity, there are really only three.

1. **A Direct Disposition.** All this means is that you are hiring the services of a licensed funeral director to send a transfer vehicle to your place of death, whether that is a hospital, a nursing home, or your own home. They will pick up the remains and transport them back to the preparation room at the funeral home, arrange for the cremation and return the ashes to you.

2. **A Memorial Service** contains everything a direct disposition contains, but the funeral establishment puts on a service, either in their own building, or in the church of your choice. Sometimes people want it to be held in a different location, such as a club that has their own facilities. It is important to note that with a memorial service, the body is not present, no casket is present, cremation has already taken place, and most often, the urn is present in lieu of a casket.

3. **A Traditional Service**: This is the type of arrangement where the casket is present. I'm not sure why, but many people are under the misconception that a traditional service is not available with cremation. The facts are that there are only two real differences between a traditional service with cremation to follow, and a traditional service with burial to follow. The first difference is that with burial, there is a funeral procession from the funeral home or church to the cemetery, and with cremation to follow, there is not, because the body has to be transported to the crematorium. The second difference is that with burial, a casket

is purchased, and the casket is buried. But with cremation, the funeral home usually provides the use of the casket for the visitation and service, and hidden inside the casket underneath the white satin lining, where no one can see, is the combustible, rigid, leak-proof container that is always necessary with cremation.

"I'm donating my body to science!"

This is what you need to know with regards to whole body donation. Medical schools, or schools of anatomy will accept body donations to train future medical professionals. It is completely different than donating organs. The body must be in very good condition and there must be a need for the body. It is important to remember that if you have a pre-paid funeral and you are accepted by a medical school, the pre-paid funeral fund will be returned to the family with interest.

SUMMARY

What do all of these things I've been talking about have in common? The greatest point of all that I've written here is that there are many ways for you to achieve wealth and grow it. An early mortgage and long-term investments can result in a free home for your loved ones to live in, money for them to live on and funds to grow even more money. They can even take the money they used to pay rent with and purchase yet more investments, so that when the third generation matures, there is a literal fortune waiting for them to inherit.

We also discussed investment vehicles such as real estate, mutual funds and term deposits, touching on various types of each, the idea being to make you aware of the choices you have moving forward. We even talked about how to protect your earning potential with disability insurance and life insurance. The chapter ended with a looked at funeral planning.

You came to Canada to make a better life for your family. This chapter can set you on the proper path to achieve what you wish. Good luck in all you do!

Declutter Your Mind for Success

ERIN MULDOON STETSON

"**M**y baggage", "your baggage", "his baggage" —phrases thrown around in casual conversation as much as an actual suitcase is thrown around by handlers at an airport. What does it mean when we talk about our "baggage?" After all, we're not actually referring to that matching set of luggage your mother bought you after college, are we? No, we are talking about the emotional and life experience "stuff" you pick up along the way; the stuff that weighs you down and makes the inside of your head hurt.

When we take a trip, our baggage literally gets heavier and messier with each souvenir we add. And, if you're like me, you can't wait to unpack and put the dirty laundry in the wash where it belongs. Similarly, in life every experience comes with emotional as well as physical stuff. Unfortunately, not all of it is as pleasurable as the mementos from vacation. Plus, when unpacking, most of us take a look at what comes out of the suitcase so we can put it where it belongs.

But, when it comes to emotional baggage, people tend to stuff it away without really looking at it. What they are doing is filling up the emotional equivalent of a classic, overstuffed closet; the one where, when you open the door, a thousand things come crashing down on your head. The one where you don't open the door except maybe a couple inches now and then to stuff more things into the dark, scary closet.

On an emotional level, that stuffing is doing you no good at all. In fact, all that clutter is not relegated to your subconscious mind. It affects all parts of your mind, as well as your body and spirit. It causes pain, disease and emotional issues. It can block you in countless ways—from achieving your potential, living authentically and manifesting abundance in your life.

Why is your mind so cluttered in the first place? It's because you've been "collecting" experiences, memories and feelings for a lifetime. Even in the womb, there may have been alarming and confusing experiences. If you had a difficult birth, or traumatic first few moments of life, the imprint of those experiences is still with you. To add insult to injury, as a baby, you may have often struggled to be understood or to have your needs met while your bumbling care givers tried to figure out if you were hungry, sleepy or needed a diaper change. How frustrating that must have been. Those early experiences went into your collection.

Think about the clutter you have collected. I suggest that, as you read this, you jot down the thoughts that pop into your head. No doubt you will start to think of your own personal clutter that is stuffed inside you somewhere. Your notes will help you when you decide to clear that clutter out. Remember, you

134

need to look at all of it squarely before you can put it away for good.

The collection of emotional clutter goes on throughout your life. In the toddler years, you stumble and fall (literally), and struggle to communicate only to be utterly misunderstood. Then, as a teen, you stumble figuratively as you try to find your way, and still find communication difficult as your values change in relation to those of parents, teachers or even your peers.

Think about it:

- A humiliating experience in class when a teacher scolded you in front of everyone.

- Someone you had a crush on treated you with contempt.

- A vicious, behind-the-back bullying campaign waged by an alleged "friend."

- A time when you were unkind or ungrateful to someone who didn't deserve it.

- The day you walked out of a store with a pack of gum you didn't pay for.

Each of these experiences is jarring. Every single one of them can disrupt the energy system in your body and mind. It's no wonder you feel so overwhelmed with the clutter.

I vividly remember something that happened when I was 12 years old. I received a scathing note from one of my "best friends" who happened to live across the street. It was poetic in its poignancy. "Erin, you think you're hot shit on a silver platter, but really you're just cold diarrhea on a paper plate!" Wow. That hurt. It's funny now —I mean really funny — and I'm so impressed with the verbiage. But at the time, I cried big tears —the kind of tears that I thought might never stop gushing. I had to re-think my whole persona. Did I really think that I was "hot shit?" And was I actually "just cold diarrhea?" I collected the anger, the sadness and the insecurity of that moment and buried it all in my mind, heart and body.

For the record, I'm not saying that any of the experiences I'm mentioning were bad, or good, for that matter. Nor am I saying that my friend in the "hot shit" story was wrong for writing that note. What I am saying is that our experiences stay with us, in one form or another, and often create disruptions in our energy systems.

Have you been able to jot down a few notes about memories of your own that may have stayed with you and created disruptions in your own life? Job struggles, relationship or parenting challenges, heartache, loss, trauma—the little things and the big things that may be stuffed away, buried, doing some damage unbeknownst to you.

All of these things go into your collection. Don't judge them. Don't judge yourself. Simply write down a "title" for the memory. We'll address it later and possibly let go of it with ease. You won't lose the memory, but merely the negative charge that is connected to it.

Now that you have started to examine your impressive collection, you can understand how it has grown exponentially over your lifetime. You can imagine how your mind has gotten cluttered. It's no wonder so many people feel weighed down, bottled up, distracted and even confused at times.

It is possible to declutter your mind if you have the proper tools. There is a process you can use to fix the effects of that build-up.

Pat yourself on the back for beginning this journey. It's going to be fun!

TAPPING

Tapping is based on Emotional Freedom Techniques (EFT). It is a relatively new discovery that has provided thousands with relief from pain, disease and emotional issues. It can alleviate the most common matters (fear of public speaking) to the most extreme (chronic debilitating back pain), and a wide array of "stuff" in between. Basically, tapping is mind/body healing. It is a combination of ancient Chinese knowledge and modern psychology.

Tapping produces a relaxation response in your body and mind and creates an emotional contentment in the present moment. It is wonderfully simple and effective, and it is accomplished by stimulating well established energy meridian points on your body.

"How do you do that?"

You do that by tapping on particular points with your fingertips while focusing on the issue at hand.

"Really?" "It's not more complicated than that?"

Yes, really. And no, it's not more complicated than that. Plus, the process is easy to memorize, and portable—you can do it anywhere. You only need your hands and your mind.

It is my goal to make this real healing easy and accessible to you. For the entrepreneur feeling overwhelmed, or the person who has dreams of starting a business but is blocked by fear, these techniques can help create such fundamental shifts that walls tumble and doors open. The healing path of body, mind and spirit lies ahead.

So how does tapping differ, say, from other energy healing modalities such as acupuncture? By focusing on the mind-body connection, EFT tapping harnesses the power of the mind and combines it with the body's energy to propel healing to a level that could not otherwise be achieved. The techniques essentially bring a psychotherapeutic element to the energy meridians long familiar to alternative healers.

The power of thought and its effects on our well-being are no longer considered theoretical. The evidence is piling up. So let's declutter your mind so that your thoughts no longer sabotage you but can have the impact you want them to!

EFT TAPPING IN ACTION

Let's look at a particular, very real scenario that will be familiar to many. I like to call it the fear of public writing. Now, we could also address the fear of public speaking or something else but, given the fact that I overcame my fear of public writing to write this chapter, it seems an apropos example. Additionally, the fear of public writing can be a huge deal for an entrepreneur, especially when you are expected to publish a blog, post on Facebook and update your website on a regular basis.

EFT tapping has the unique ability to handle your fears and turn them into calm cool action. Whether you feel paralyzed at the thought of doing an activity like writing, or are shy about sharing what you've already written, EFT tapping can help put those fears in check.

For example, have you hesitated to write a book because of your anxiety about the fact that the dreaded written word can never be erased? It will be "out there" speaking for you, for all time. If you are like I was, that thought paralyzes you. But here I am, writing this. And enjoying it, I might add. How am I able to face my fears so courageously?

As I mentioned above, the answer is quite simple and incredibly revolutionary. I can't wait to share this fabulous secret with you. Tap along with me. You won't be sorry. Then we can high five on the other side of this silly fear that's holding you back from your greatness.

EFT IN A NUTSHELL

The body contains a network of energy points and energy channels — actual locations that can be accessed through tapping. In addition to the physical act of tapping on these specific points, EFT involves the use of words. The power of words, of language, to channel and manifest intention is hardly in question any more. So with EFT, you will use words first to acknowledge the details of the negative — the big pieces of junk cluttering your mind.

Looking at them and facing them is the first step to releasing the junk you've been shoving into your suitcase for so long. Finally, positive language is used to manifest what you want to bring into your life after you've released the unwanted clutter through tapping.

So, let's return to our hypothetical case of a person (maybe you) who is afraid to write. This fear is getting in the way of your business, your success and your ability to create abundance in your life. Below are the simple steps that I would walk you through if you were this hypothetical person. In no time, you would be writing and publishing.

STEP 1

Close your eyes and think about what is holding you back from writing and publishing that book or updating your blog. Once you have something specific in mind, give it a number on a scale of 0-10, ten being the most intense. If you have many things running through your mind, write them down and start with the one specific issue that has the highest intensity. Think of it as the biggest piece of junk in that closet—the one that might actually knock you out if it fell on your head. Give that piece of junk a "title"—you don't need to write down the whole sordid history or explanation of the issue, just its title. The number you assign to that issue is extremely important. It allows you to compare how you feel before and after tapping.

For example, you may be thinking: "What if my ex reads this and thinks, 'what the %&*# is she writing about? Why was I ever with that chick? What a weirdo!'" Or perhaps you are thinking, "No one who reads this will ever want to talk to me, meet me or hire me. I'll be ruined."

Your title for this piece of mental debris might be: Fear of Rejection. Maybe it earns a level of 8, 9 or even 10, depending on how paralyzing it is. (You insert whichever number makes sense for how you feel in the present moment.)

STEP 2

Tap continuously with your fingers on each of the following spots while repeating the corresponding phrases out loud. (If you think a diagram might be helpful, please visit http://taponit.com.)

Karate Chop Spot (this is the place on the side of your hand you would use if you were to use a karate chop to break a piece of wood): Tap continuously with four fingers on that spot while saying the following phrase three times aloud: "Even though I am afraid of being judged and rejected [insert here: by my ex or by future clients] for what I write, I'm still a really good person."

- **Eyebrow point** (this is the beginning of your eyebrow closest to your nose): Tap continuously with two fingers at that spot and repeat the following phrase: "I'm afraid that my [ex or future client] is going to judge me and my writing in a negative way."

- **Side of eye** (this is the bone bordering the outside corner of your eye): Tap continuously with two fingers on that spot and repeat the following phrase: "What if my [ex or future client] reads what I wrote and thinks I'm a terrible writer?"

- **Under the eye** (about 1/2 inch below the eye on the bone): Tap continuously with two fingers, saying: "I'm nervous to put myself out there. I will be laughed at."

- **Under the nose** (this is the philtrum: the small indentation between the bottom of your nose and the top of your upper lip): Tap continuously with two fingers on that spot while you say: "I'm afraid that someone [my ex or a judgmental future client] is going to read my writing if I put it out there."

- **Chin** (the spot inside the indentation midway between the bottom of your chin and your lower lip): Tap continuously with two fingers on that spot and say: "I'm not sure if I can handle the embarrassment of having my writing judged by [my ex, a future client] or anyone else for that matter."

- **Collarbone**: Tap continuously with four fingers along your collarbone towards your breast bone. Say these words: "I'm not ready to have my thoughts and ideas critiqued and ridiculed."

- **Under arm** (four inches below your armpit, on the side of your body): Tap continuously with four fingers: "I'm nervous that [my ex or a future client] will read what I'm writing and make fun of me."

- **Crown of head**: Tap continuously with all five fingers in a circular motion on the top of your head: "I'm afraid that [my ex or anyone] is going to read my writing and laugh at me."

- **Eyebrow point**: "I'm okay now."

- **Side of eye**: "I can relax now."

- **Under the eye**: "I am calm and relaxed."

- **Under the nose**: "My confidence is growing."

- **Chin**: "I am feeling more and more confident about my writing."

- **Collarbone**: "I am excited to write an awesome [book, article, blog]."

- **Under arm**: "I can't wait to write my [book, article, blog]."

- **Top of head**: "I'm ready to write and publish an amazing [book, article, blog]."

When you are done, take a deep breath and hold it. Then let it out in a slow, smooth exhalation.

STEP 3

After completing the tapping and repetitions, reassess the intensity of your feelings about the topic (in this case, public writing), using the scale you used originally, from 0 to 10, with ten being the strongest. Write down your response, the number and something about how you feel. Comment about whether there were any qualitative changes to the way you view or feel about the topic. If your number is still high, then repeat the process.

Be clear in acknowledging any change. For example, "After tapping, my fear of rejection and judgment regarding my writing from [my ex or future clients] is at about a level two, down significantly from my previous level of eight."

The three steps outlined above are how you use EFT to overcome your fear of public writing. You can use the same format to cope with other issues that are holding you back. The phrases that you use in your repetitions during tapping will vary according to what you are trying to release. Here are some examples:

- **Karate Chop Spot**: "Even though I'm afraid that my family will disown me because what I want to write about is too off the grid for them, I have confidence and love. I forgive them for their potential judgments." Repeat three times.

- **Karate Chop Spot**: "Even though I fear that my ideas will change one day, and what I write will be 'out there' forever, reminding me of how foolish I was, I deeply and completely love and accept myself."

- **Karate Chop Spot**: "Even though my writing isn't perfect, it's a work in progress that never seems to end. I am whole, and complete, and fabulous just as I am right now, and so is my writing."

- **Karate Chop Spot**: "Even though I feel as if I don't have time to write, I am willing to make changes in my life because I deeply and completely love and accept myself."

The intended and very real outcome of EFT tapping in this circumstance is increased self-confidence. Whether it is your writing or something else that is standing in your way, your confidence will grow exponentially the more you tap. You will laugh at your previous fears. To use our example of fearing the reaction of your ex, once you have utilized EFT tapping, you might assume that, should he read your writing, he'll wonder how he ever let someone like you get away!

Our fears about what might happen are often times more intense than any actual, potential outcome. Tapping creates equilibrium between that fear and what is real. It will allow you to gain a calm, cool perspective regarding the debris that was weighing you down by cluttering up your suitcase or your closet –in other words, your mind!

Decluttering your mind through EFT tapping applies to literally any aspect of your life. It can help you find fulfillment, success, and enjoyment in any arena: relationships, money, body image, health etc. Starting with identifying what is holding you back, seeing it for what it is and then releasing it, you ultimately replace it with something positive that will help you move forward.

The things that are holding you back are all that junk we talked about earlier: Fears or objections (the "I can't" mentality), obstacles — perceived or real (time, logistics) — and ultimately your "story" – the belief system that holds you where you are instead of helping you get to where you want to be.

The process that works for your mind can also be used to declutter your body. There is a holistic connection between and among mind, body and spirit, which means that detoxing one will help you connect with the others to live your best life.

In using EFT techniques for the spirit, you will address matters of perspective, outlook and attitude. The law of attraction is essentially at work every time you succumb to fear or, conversely, feel optimistic. When you fear an outcome and fixate on that fear, you are focusing on what is essentially a belief system based on fear. Your mind, as well as your actions, reflects that belief system and you will manifest the very things you are afraid of.

When you can tap on and release the fear, you can recreate a belief system based on positive emotions, optimism and confidence. You become that person and your every action reflects those new beliefs.

So what does this mean for you? It means that EFT tapping can bring you more comfort, love and enjoyment in life. It can help you rid yourself of the heavy baggage and clutter that get in the way of being your most successful self.

To learn more about the benefits of tapping, please visit http://taponit.com.

Bringing Balance
to Your Life

DENNIS GARRIDO

When I woke up in the hospital staring up into the terrified eyes of someone I cared about, after my second cardiac arrest in one year, I knew that things had to change in my life. Especially because I was only in my twenties at the time.

Everything in my life was out of balance. Obviously, physically because I was lying in the emergency room, but more importantly my mind, emotions, and spirit were completely out of whack, and that had taken a toll on my body.

Now you may be wondering how someone so young could have had two cardiac arrests before the age of 30? It won't be hard to imagine once I share my story with you. I wish I could tell you that I had a great upbringing, one filled with laughter and love, but it wasn't.

At age eleven I was removed from my parent's home by The Children's Aid Society because they deemed my parents unfit to raise me. During that time, I went through a whirlwind of emotions. A part of me was happy that change was finally occurring, because clearly at that point, the way things were, wasn't working at all.

Another part of me felt fear because of the unknown. I didn't know exactly where I would be living, nor did I know for sure what my group & foster homes would be like, what the other kids would be like, what the living conditions would be like, how far or close I'd be to my family and hometown, etc. Essentially, I wasn't 100% certain nor 100% convinced that I was going into better circumstances.

Also, I felt sad, since I wouldn't see my parents or siblings anymore, nor my home town and many of the people whom I'd see on a regular basis; everything FAMILIAR would be gone! Lastly, I felt angry, that it had come to me being removed from my parent's house, away from those who were in my life for all those years. As twisted and messed up as it may be, I was angry that I was leaving a life that I had become accustomed to and felt somewhat comfortable in (comfortable in comparison to the unknown that lay ahead); and most of all, angry that I was leaving FAMILIARITY!!!!

Please understand me, I am no longer angry at my parents, and you shouldn't be either. They did the best they could, but when you are broken yourself, unless you find a way out, you will repeat what had been bestowed on you from the previous generations. I can be thankful because what I went through helped create the person I am today and as a coach, it gives me great empathy and understanding to be able to help others. So, don't feel sorry for me because even though my life had a rough start, I get to choose the rest of it and it is going to be GREAT!!!

THE NEXT SEVEN YEARS OF MY LIFE

For the next seven years until I turned 18, I was bounced from foster/group home to foster/group home. I rarely spent more than three months at any one place, and it caused some major emotional setbacks that took me a long time to overcome.

One of the biggest negative emotional setbacks was again to do with familiarity. As I spent time with those at my new home, seeing them every day and coming to know them personally; I naturally formed a connection/ friendship with them. It seemed that no sooner had I done that; they were removed from my life. People whom I really liked (a few of them, whom I loved), ALL GONE!!! Which basically solidified my already ingrained defence mechanism of keeping distant from others; not allowing anyone to get close enough to form any connection with me.

Inevitably, this made it very difficult for me to form any type of relationship with anyone. School and extracurricular activities were hard because I never knew how long I would be staying in one place. What was the point of making friends if I could never keep them? It was a lot easier to keep my distance than to reach out yet again and have everything torn away from me.

Eventually, I started to tear down the wall that prevented me from getting too close to anyone. To this day, the negative emotional setbacks I experienced, still affect me to some degree; though I CHOOSE not to allow them to prevent me from forming meaningful relationships!

THE DARKEST TIME OF MY LIFE

All that change led to one of the darkest periods of my life. Emotionally and mentally I had shut down and could no longer function. Life was so hard. Even things that were simple, now became agonizingly difficult and it hit the point where I didn't want to live anymore. What was the use of carrying on in this horrible life when there wasn't any hope of it changing?

My life began to narrow down to one permanent solution, and that was to end it all by committing suicide. I just couldn't handle life anymore, but I truly believe that Almighty God, the universe or whatever you want to call it, had a bigger plan for me. Even though I tried several times, I just couldn't die!!! Because of those attempts, I ended up in psychiatric institutions, a few times.

It finally came to the point where I was tired of trying to die, I was tired of institutions and I was weary from all the self-harm, and so I came to a decision. I guess you could say that it was a turning point in my life; I wasn't going to attempt suicide anymore. I wasn't sure what to do because my circumstances hadn't changed, but I was willing to look for options. That was the beginning point of change in my life. The will to live!!!

IT DIDN'T GET BETTER RIGHT AWAY

Life is a journey with twists, hills, and valleys of varying shapes and sizes, with occasional points where you make decisions that put you on a different path. The determination not to kill myself had set me on a new road, but I still didn't know what to do or which way to go. It was slow going as I fumbled my way through, but at least I was moving forward!!!

At age 18 I was no longer in the custody of The Children's Aid Society, so, I moved back with my parents, which was the perfect testing grounds for me to apply the life lessons I had learned so far. You would be amazed by how much maturity one can have at 18 when you have been through what I have. It wasn't easy, and it was hard work, but I managed to re-establish a relationship with my parents and not only complete high school, but also graduate from post-secondary schooling.

One of the things I had decided to do was get my student loans paid off in the six-month grace period, which I managed to do; but in doing so, I pushed myself way beyond my physical limits which brought on the first cardiac arrest.

You would think I would have learned from that first experience, but I didn't, and less than a year later we are back to the beginning of this chapter waking up in the hospital from my second one.

This time I learned my lesson and chose a different path, but I still didn't know how to achieve what I needed. For so long I had lived in imbalance, that I didn't know where to start, but the catalyst for change was just around the corner.

I FINALLY REALIZED WHAT BALANCE WAS

Believe it or not, it is the simplest things that can bring about the most profound changes in life. My search for balance in my life had begun, and it is amazing how the answer came; by a knock at my door one day.

That day I was busy working on something, so when the first knock came, I ignored it. It was only after a couple of rings of the doorbell that I finally decided that I would answer it. There was a well-dressed gentleman at the door and even though I don't remember most of what he said, one thing became clear, I was missing an essential element to finding the balance I craved. Now, I knew what it was. You can only find balance when you address ALL the areas of your life, and I had been missing one. The spiritual side.

It is amazing what happens when you finally have all the pieces together. As I started to study the Bible, I finally could build a solid spiritual foundation, that enabled me to re-evaluate things in my life, and thus, put a plan together to create balance in my life. In the rest of this chapter, I am going to share with you what I learned.

Just before I do that, I do want to mention one thing. All of this is a process. Can I say that I am 100% balanced in my life? No, but when I started at 3-4% and then jumped to 85%, I think that is very good growth. It's difficult to attain 100% balance in every aspect of one's life, that is why even the most successful people keep learning and growing. So, the goal is not perfection, but growth. As long as you are continuing to move forward, that is all that matters.

7 STEPS TO BRING BALANCE TO YOUR LIFE

Here's one of the things that I have learned about bringing balance to your life. In some ways, it is easy. The steps I am going to teach you are simple to understand. The hard part is training yourself to be aware of it every day and live by it. The good thing is, though it may be hard at first, the more you practice it, the easier it gets.

STEP 1

Ask yourself, "What are my priorities in life?" You want to look at it from all aspects of your life, personal and professional. In terms of personal that includes goals physically, emotionally, mentally, spiritually, relationships (such as your spouse or significant other), family and friends. You want to look at it from the point of what you need and what you want. For each one, you should have one to two priorities.

In terms of professional, they can include your current work situation and areas of improvement there, plus plan for your future. Put down both needs and wants.

	NEEDS	WANTS
P E R S O N A L		
P R O F E S S I O N A L		

STEP 2

Look at your needs column. What are the most important priorities personally and professionally? It is important that you only start out working on a few at a time. If you try to do everything at once, you will become overwhelmed and quit. Then, figure out the things you need to do to get those needs met.

STEP 3

Now go through your wants and do the same thing as Step 2 above. Don't overlook this. Part of having balance in life is having both your needs and wants met. Obviously, your needs are more important, but without the wants, you give up hope.

STEP 4

Set up a timeline for those needs to be accomplished. What are you going to do today, this week, this month, this year, and in the next five years to bring yourself to reach those priorities?

STEP 5

Do the same thing for your wants. Set up your timeline of completion.

STEP 6

DO THE ACTIONS. Here is where the rubber meets the road. You can plan and plan and plan, but if there is no action involved you will be in the same place, with the same problems, five years from now.

STEP 7

Re-evaluate. Every few months go back through this whole process again.

As you grow and change, so will your priorities, your needs and your wants.

THE BEST WAY TO ACCOMPLISH THIS

Very rarely can a person accomplish this alone. Have you ever heard the saying, "You can't see the forest for the trees?" That is what happens in our lives. We get so caught up in the unimportant things right in front of us, that we miss the big picture and we don't recognize growth when it occurs.

Now, you do have several options. One is to have family members try to help you through this. While you do need their support, they are usually looking at the same trees you are and can miss things.

Two, you can go to friends for help. They do tend to see more of the big picture, but many times they can't give you the encouragement and motivation you need at times to get past yourself.

Three, you work with a professional who knows how to help you bring balance to your life. They can come alongside of you and guide you to the quickest path to success because there will be obstacles that try to stop you. Did I forget to mention that?

No road to balance is smooth; little pebbles will get into your shoes to irritate you and take your focus off your goals. Barriers will be put up that you will have to learn how to go over, under, around or through. People will get in your way and tell you that it is the wrong road to take and you should follow them. All sorts of things will try to keep you from what you want.

Coaches are keen observers who can not only help you with what is going on right now, but they have been down your road and they know what is up ahead and can keep you moving forward, even when everything is telling you to stop.

That is what I'm offering to be for you. Let me help you on your path to balance in your life. I have been on both sides of the coin, and I can guide you through the roughest parts. I can relate to what you are feeling and am more than willing to help you navigate this wonderful thing called life.

First of all, if you would like more information on how to start this process, you can pre-order my upcoming book at www.dennisgarrido.com Second, you can email me at dennis@dennisgarrido.com and request your free 15-minute phone consultation where we can discuss your situation and see if we are a good fit for each other. Third, maybe you realize more people need to hear this message. I am also available to speak to groups and conferences. If so, just send me an email, and we can arrange a time to speak.

No matter what you decide, know this. You can achieve balance in your life. It is possible. I can tell you that it has been worth everything I went through to get to this point. The peace I experience now, compared to the chaos I lived before, is so amazing and I wish the same for you.

Don't miss out. Make the choice to change your life today, and I guarantee that you won't regret it!!!

Motivation Does Activate and Sustain Behaviour

How to Bring Results in Life and Business

JULIE HOGBIN

B efore we talk about motivation in any great detail, it would be a good idea to cover the basics about what motivation really is. There are many, many, theories and huge amounts of research has been conducted on the subject over many decades. To be honest, with all the information out there it can be confusing as to what it all means.

One thing is for sure, one theory — one piece of information — does not cover it all as each researcher has their own bent and interpretation on the subject. It is when you are able to link it all together that it starts to make sense and you are able to do something with the information to help yourself.

I have researched, read about, practiced, and taught this subject to over 20,000 Leaders in Life, Business and the Entrepreneur market, both one-on-one and in small groups for very nearly three decades, and I am still learning.

This chapter is based around my knowledge, my interpretation, and a definition of Motivation that I have worked with for a long time. I have neither found nor developed a better definition — yet!

"Motivation is a conscious or unconscious driving force that arouses and directs action towards the achievement of a desired goal."

ClaimYourDestiny.global   #ConsciousLeadership

So, what does this mean in reality? It means that we are motivated by internal and external factors and that sometimes we know what those factors are and sometimes we don't: Our actions and thoughts are both conscious and unconscious in nature. It also means that the motives provoke a reaction and an action that help us 'get' something we want — a goal — and as a driving force they are powerful.

So my 1st questions to you are:

- What is your goal?

- What are you working towards?

- How many goals do you have?

- What is driving you?

- How conscious are you?

Motivation is an internal force; we are the only ones who can motivate us. Motivation can be affected by external influences. Ultimately it is us, and only us, that make the decision to do or not to do something. Nobody can make you feel or do anything! It is your absolute choice to capitulate and do, or to resist and not do.

We make the decision based on the information we have at the time and how confident we feel. There are many emotions and personal characteristics that come into play when we are talking about motivation and all that entails.

When we say that others motivate us what it really means is that they have created an environment that inspires us to do something. We make the decision out of fear in some cases, because we know it makes sense in other cases, because we aspire to be like the individual, or, more simply, just because we want to.

For you, and everybody else, your desired goal always provides you with a positive outcome. It gives you something you want even if that want is unconsciously driven. For others viewing it from their perspective, that outcome may be viewed as negative.

Let me explain what I mean with a couple of examples.

Addicts of any description do whatever it takes to fuel their need. They are achieving their desired outcome with more alcohol, more food, less food, more drugs, or just more of something, and they will go to extreme lengths to get it, such as selling personal and other people's belongings, lying and deceiving, going into debt and stealing.

Someone comes home with great intent of doing some research, maybe to write a book or to do some personal development such as going to the gym, and they end up sitting in front of the TV for hours with a bottle of wine. What is their driving force? We may not understand it as the viewer but there is definitely one for the person being observed.

Let's look at a couple of positive examples with a more generally accepted encouraging outcome.

A young person decides what they want to achieve in their life. They study like crazy to get the grades required to get to the top university and to study in a class of four with the top professor in their subject matter field, and they achieve it.

An individual from an underprivileged background wants to change their life, achieve greater things than have ever been achieved in their family, and become independently wealthy, and they are successful in achieving their goals.

Now for every example shared the opposite can be true as well. Not everybody becomes an addict, not everyone slouches in front of the TV, not every student achieves their potential, and not every underprivileged individual becomes independently wealthy.

"Everything you do is goal-driven. Everything you do is because you want the end result — whatever that end result may be!"

ClaimYourDestiny.global   #ConsciousLeadership

The examples are all based on how motivated the individual is to achieve their goal. Now if you know your goal consciously, can keep it in focus and resist the temptation of your old ways, you can achieve marvellous results.

The rest of this chapter will look at what drives you and how you can change your habits and behaviours over a period both short and long term, with the aim to achieve whatever it is you want.

I reference no theory in this chapter. There are many to read and learn which are of use to us all intellectually and unless the theory is practically applied and interpreted into reality all they remain are theories. I have spent decades interpreting theories into real life behaviours that make a difference for the better.

A few more questions for you to think about first.

- What are your drivers?

- What are your values?

- What is your risk tolerance?

- How much do you want to fit in with the 'norm' of your social group?

- How much do you really want, on a scale of 1 to 10, the thing it is you are aiming to achieve?

- How comfortable are you with change?

There are a lot more questions to ask but these will start you on the journey to understand your own motivators.

"Your motives create your habits, for good and bad, as they are your driving force."

ClaimYourDestiny.global   #ConsciousLeadership

There is so much information coming at us on a minute by minute basis. We make thousands upon thousands of decisions every day — so many in fact, we cannot be conscious of all the decisions, to do or not to do something, that we do make. We would be completely overwhelmed if we did.

So what do we do? We create patterns of behaviour that we do not have to think about, as it is quicker that way, to achieve our outcomes. We create habits that get us what we want in the easiest manner.

"Your habits have created your behaviour through your values, beliefs, and attitudes."

ClaimYourDestiny.global   #ConsciousLeadership

HABITS

Habits are a set of thoughts, behaviours, and ways of being that are developed through repeated behaviour. Habits are formed from the moment we become aware that there is a 'norm' of how to do things. Some we pick up from our parents, guardians, siblings, and influential individuals around us at a very early age. Others we develop for ourselves through the maturing process.

What is seen what is known

Conscious

Easily recoverable

Preconscious

Unconscious
Creates us!
Drives us!
Influences us!

What is unseen
What is unknown

© JulieHogbin.com

"Look to your parents for your beliefs about the world and yourself – you may be amazed at the similarities."

ClaimYourDestiny.global   #ConsciousLeadership

Once habits are created they can be difficult to break. To break a habit, we must consciously think about doing something different and then do it — which can equal hard work and being uncomfortable.

The thing is, we can all break habits if we really want to. BUT (and there is a big BUT) the unconscious part of our being is there to keep us safe. Any change and it may feel we are under threat and revert quickly to the old ways.

"Talk to your unconscious and ask its permission if you want to change some deep held habits and motivations to do things in a new way."

"Sounds a bit weird? Well it works, try it for yourself."

ClaimYourDestiny.global   #ConsciousLeadership

VALUES

Your values are a central part of who you are and who you want to be. By becoming more aware of these driving motivators in your life, you can use them as a guide to make the best choice in any situation.

Your decisions and actions, when in line with your values, will be easy to make and put into practice. If you are attempting to do something that is not held as a value to you, you will find it harder to do and, potentially, you will be in conflict with yourself.

Here is an example. If one of your values is honesty and you are in a relationship, business or personal, with someone who you know tells untruths, how hard will you find it to trust them? What will this do to your behaviour and your motivation within the relationship?

Values can be worked with, reordered, and installed — so do not lose hope. I personally have needed to work hard on my value regarding money. To say the least, it was slightly askew!

ATTITUDES

Your attitude is a predisposition to respond either negatively or positively towards an idea, object, person, or situation. It is the way you feel about something or someone. It can also be a particular feeling or opinion. It is seen as a conscious behaviour but will come from an unconscious driver.

Your attitude evolves as a result of your beliefs and values and will influence:

- Your choice of action and behaviour

- Your response to challenges

- Your response to incentives

- Your response to a word

- Your response to someone trying to help you

We all have an attitude — we cannot not have one. Generally, when it is said someone has an attitude it is meant as a negative opinion, but attitudes are drivers for good as well. It is just a common adaptation of a word which is more often linked to negativity.

As with anything else we do, our attitude is a choice we make. My choice, and I trust yours as you are reading this book, is to start each day with a positive attitude — it soon becomes a habit.

If you want to change something in your life, surround yourself with those who are on the same path or learn from those who have already done the 'thing' that you want to do. Attitudes are contagious so eradicate those personally held by yourself and those that are owned by people that may be in your circle who aren't helping you. If you don't know what your attitudes are, ask someone for feedback who will tell you the truth.

Also carefully study your close associates to make your own decisions on who stays with you on your journey and who leaves, their attitudes can be contagious. Look at the relationships that are in your life and acknowledge whether they are supporting you or hindering you. Decisions then can be made from a realistic position of what you want to do.

SOCIAL INTELLIGENCE

Social intelligence indicates that portions of our knowledge acquisition can be directly related to observing others within the context of social interactions, experiences and media influences.

So what does this mean to all of us? Basically, it means that if we see something that is rewarded, we copy it so that we get rewarded. We achieve the same result as we have observed, therefore we have achieved our result, which was our goal. There is far more to it but that's the basic concept. We learn by example from others.

So who do we copy? We copy those close to us and we adopt behaviours to fit into the crowd and belong. As we get older, we copy those who we admire or those who we aspire to be like. We develop a sense of self and become more aware of what it is we want. We begin to lead rather than follow — well some of us do and I expect you are a leader since you are reading this book! Join my Facebook group for more, https://www.facebook.com/groups/ClaimYourDestiny/

We are motivated to belong to a group with a certain set of characteristics. That could be because it is what we want or it can be because we know no different. It can be through peer pressure or choice, but whichever route we take it is ultimately our choice!

Join my Facebook group for more, https://www.facebook.com/groups/ClaimYourDestiny/

It is these drivers of behaviour that make you act differently from, or the same as, others in any given situation. So, by understanding these drivers, you

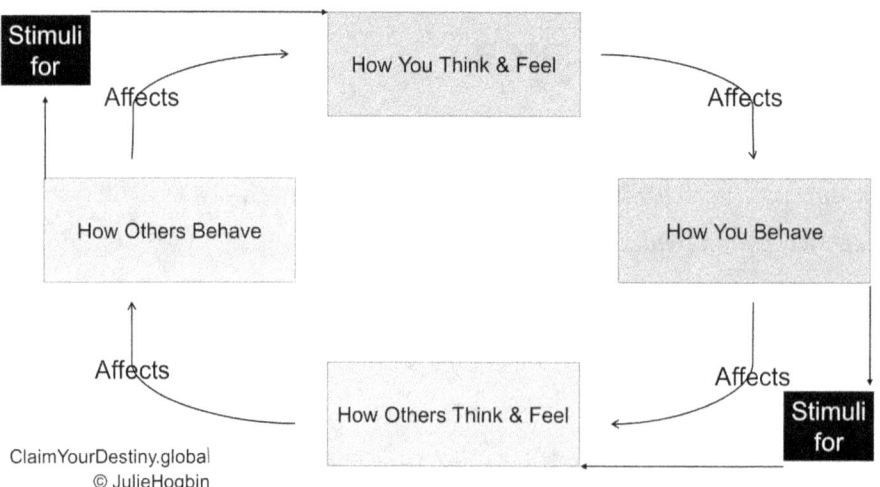

can better understand why you do the things you do. The skill is not only to understand your conscious needs, but also those that are unconscious in nature.

"In the choice between changing one's mind and proving there's no need to do so, most people get busy on the proof."

-John Kenneth Galbraith

SELF-PERCEPTION

Self-perception is the belief or disbelief in our own capabilities to achieve a goal or an outcome. These beliefs provide the foundation for human motivation, well-being, and personal accomplishment. This is because unless you believe that your actions can produce the outcomes you desire, you will have little incentive to act or to persevere in the face of difficulties.

Of course, human functioning is influenced by many factors. The success or failure you experience as you engage the countless tasks that comprise your life naturally influences the many decisions you must make. Also, the knowledge and skills you possess will certainly play critical roles in what you choose to do and not do.

"People's level of motivation, emotional states, and actions are based more on what they believe than on what is objectively true. For this reason, how you behave can often be better predicted by the beliefs you hold about your capabilities than by what you are actually capable of accomplishing."

ClaimYourDestiny.global   #ConsciousLeadership

You only need to watch one of the reality TV shows to see how clearly some people are deluded about their own abilities. The opposite is also true — you talk to someone who you know is gifted and they think and believe the complete opposite.

Our upbringing and early influencers, or even a recent happening, have a huge part to play in how and what we believe about ourselves. The great news though is whatever has happened in the past does not have to happen in our future.

These perceptions help determine what you do with the knowledge and skills you have. They also explain why your behaviours are sometimes not matched to your actual capabilities and why your behaviour may differ widely from somebody else, even when you have similar knowledge and skills.

For example, many talented people suffer frequent (and sometimes debilitating) bouts of self-doubt about capabilities they clearly possess, just as many individuals are confident about what they can accomplish despite possessing a modest repertoire of skills. Belief and reality are seldom perfectly matched, and individuals are typically guided by their beliefs when they engage the world.

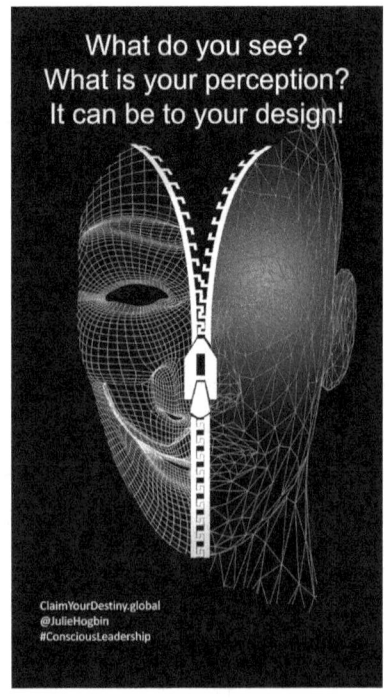

As a consequence, your accomplishments are generally better predicted by your self-perception than by your previous achievements, knowledge, or skills. Of course, no amount of confidence or self-appreciation can produce success when requisite skills and knowledge are absent.

168

"Skills and knowledge can all be gained if you want them enough and you find the right mentor to teach you."

ClaimYourDestiny.global   #ConsciousLeadership

COLLECTIVE PERCEPTION

Because individuals operate collectively as well as individually, self-perception is both a personal and a social construct. Collective systems develop a sense of collective effectiveness, it can create the group's shared belief in its capability to attain goals and accomplish desired tasks.

One brain is one but the collective brainpower of a group equals more than the sum of its parts — it's the adage $1+1=3$ or $2+2=5$. However, this is only true when the collective works together in harmony with the same aim. If members of the collective are working against each other one brain doesn't even equate to one — it will function at a lesser capability, as will the individual as they will be experiencing conflict.

For example, organisations develop collective beliefs about the capability of their salesforce to perform, of their managers to teach and otherwise enhance the lives of their workforce, and of their administrators and policymakers to create environments conducive to these tasks. Organisations, as well as individuals, also create beliefs that are not positive — they cannot gain additional sales, clients, revenue, etc. Collectiveness creates a culture which needs to be managed.

Organisations with a strong sense of positive collective perception exercise empowering and vitalising influences over their employees. These effects are evident in their results.

The power of others' attitudes (as mentioned previously) are contagious and will affect your motivation. If you are in the company of a high sender of negative emotion, you will be affected. If you are in the company of a high sender of positivity, it will be less influential.

As the saying goes, it only takes one bad apple to spoil the barrel.

Weed out the bad apples and your motivation will improve. Take on more of the good apples that are doing the same thing that you want to do and your motivation will improve by leaps and bounds.

CHOICES

Only you can justify the choices you make and most of you will make your choices in reference to past experiences rather than future opportunities. Change how you think and you will change your future.

> *"The definition of insanity is doing the same thing over and over again and expecting a different result."*
>
> – Albert Einstein

How do you change to get a different result? It's easy, think differently and take different actions. Open your mind and your being to possibilities; your past does not have to equal your future. With #ConsciousLeadership it can all change.

Every thought, every action, and every decision you make takes you closer to, or further away, from where you want to be. The smallest of decisions compounded over time creates massive change. Rather than attempt to make a huge change overnight, which can be scary and overwhelming, make small incremental changes that lead you towards your goal.

What do I mean? 5 minutes exercise a day wont make much difference if you do or don't do it BUT 5 minutes everyday will. A cake on one day wont make much difference to your health BUT a cake every day will (in the wrong direction). Delaying cutting the lawn for one day wont make much difference BUT delaying every day will.

Even doing nothing takes you further away because everything else is moving forward. The skills of yesteryear will not suffice in the next year. Think about how technology changes. If you haven't kept up with the last change you will soon be a very long way behind!

Sometimes, it can be a life-changing event that allows you to make the decision to do something immediately that you have tried before and failed at. A friend of mine, when diagnosed with cancer, stopped smoking overnight after 40 years. Please do not leave it until that type of thing happens before you change. Take on board #ConsciousLeadership now and change your life for the better, it is your choice!

Start to work now on different decisions for what you want and need:

- Why wait to be taken through a disciplinary process at work before you improve your skills or performance?

- Why wait until you are so over or underweight before you change your nutrition intake?

- Why wait until you cannot walk upstairs without puffing before you increase your fitness level?

- Why wait until you are close to retirement to think about how much money you need to live on and enjoy your retirement?

Through reading, applying, and practicing the experiences of others, you can learn what has worked for those before you, and you can apply those principles in your own life.

Motivational states are directive, they guide behaviours toward satisfying specific goals or specific needs. Do you have clearly defined goals? If you don't, sit down now, identify what it is you really want or need, and write that down. Then create a plan of how you will achieve it. This will provide you with motivation to do things differently.

If you want more information on how to this, I can highly recommend my book 'The Life Changing Magic of Setting Goals'. It is available from Amazon or through ClaimYourDestiny.global

"Change begins with your awareness that your beliefs are a choice; all beliefs, conscious or unconscious, are based on a choice."

ClaimYourDestiny.global   #ConsciousLeadership

There are a myriad of choices to be made all of the time. If you choose a different way to do something, gather information that allows you to make an educated choice for action. Do your research and due diligence and pick the best solution for you.

This will enhance your confidence, create new knowledge, quieten the inner doubting voice, match your values, enhance your beliefs, or question them to bolster your attitude.

This will allow you to convince your unconscious that you are looking after it and it will help you. Provide your unconscious with the reason why you are making alternate choices to that of the past and it will support you all the way.

DELAYED GRATIFICATION

There have been many studies done related to the benefits of delayed gratification. What does this really mean? It means living with the future in mind rather than the present.

In this world of instant gratification, keeping up with the Joneses, wearing the right designer labels, being influenced by adverts that say you must have this face cream and that aftershave, feeling like your holidays must become bigger and more expensive, having to change your car every two years, etc. It can be hard to resist the instant temptation, to be outside the norm, or to exclude yourself from your friends' activities.

In the moment, sometimes it can seem obvious to take the reward, and worry about the future in the future.

Your choice is dependent on your goals, your drivers, your beliefs (and how strong they are), and how strong your will to resist temptation is.

If you can recognise when you have an opportunity for a larger or more important reward, it shows you know the difference between your needs and your wants. When you can recognise these situations, there are key terms you must think of.

Patience, will, and self-control are all characteristics of people who are masters of their environment. One common challenge is postponing immediate gratification in the pursuit of long-term goals. Delayed gratification is the process of transcending immediate temptations to achieve long-term goals.

Knowing how to create, manage, and control your goals is the first step towards completing the things you want most in life; with a goal, we engage our brain to work toward it.

Think of goals as roadmaps designed to keep you on target. They make the experience and the journey possible and more enjoyable. They, in fact, become priorities that drive our actions. They become motivators.

Let me ask you once again:

- What are your long-term goals?
  And for some of you

- What are your short-term goals?

If you do not have goals sit down now and plan them for yourself, tell yourself and others they are important, write them down and believe you are worthy of them and you will achieve them. Focus on them and they will become a reality

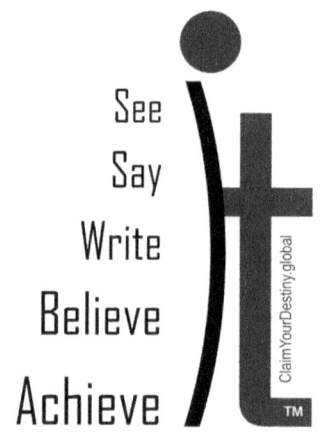

See
Say
Write
Believe
Achieve

ClaimYourDestiny.global

™

THE POWER OF QUESTIONS

Questions, when constructed in the right way, are the most powerful way

to access your beliefs. And this works irrespective of who asks the question. Ask yourself a question and your mind will do its best to provide you with an answer. The better your question, the better the answer.

Do you want to spend the rest of your life figuring out how to get the things you desire, or would you rather put all the guesswork behind you and get down to the fun of building an out-of-this-world lifestyle? Easy choice, right? Then do yourself a favour: suspend your disbelief, lower your shields, and try a simple way of improving your life.

Identify someone you respect who's already experiencing what you're after, find out what questions they habitually ask themselves to achieve those experiences, then use those questions yourself.

This is a globally powerful approach to success that can get you the things you want more quickly than anything else I've discovered. The habitual questions that others ask themselves when asked by yourself, to yourself can transform your life. You don't even need to understand how it all works really, although the answer's quite simple:

"When you change your habitual questions, you change your beliefs, when you change your beliefs, you change your actions, when you change your actions you change your results."

ClaimYourDestiny.global   #ConsciousLeadership

Try it! Take the time to prove to yourself that it works, that it can change the level of pain and pleasure in your life. If you like the results, keep using the questions you've discovered until they become second nature. Do this and you won't care about the why's and the wherefore's. You'll be too busy! You'll have learned firsthand there's nothing more powerful than a good question followed by action.

Ask different questions, and you will end up thinking different thoughts, saying different words, taking different actions, and getting different results. When you go one step further by modeling the questions of successful people, you're helping to ensure that the different results you're pursuing are also good results. In other words, you've done everything you can to arrive at a different place — a good place — to develop different beliefs, which are also profitable beliefs, and to become a different person who is more like the people you admire.

FOCUS

So what does all this mean really?

It means that by looking at why you do what you do and the beliefs behind that, you can basically change the thoughts and motives that direct your behaviour so that you achieve a different result, start a new job, get a promotion, create your own business, leave a relationship, start a relationship, have that difficult conversation, learn to swim, fly a plane, or simply eat a new food; the list is endless.

It is your choice completely — where your focus goes your energy flows — so change your focus to change your results.

Some of our important choices have a timeline. If you delay a decision, the opportunity is gone forever. Sometimes your doubts will stop you from making a choice that involves change and an opportunity may be missed. If you really truly want to change, start now — now is as good a time as any.

Create and ClaimYourDestiny.global through #ConsciousLeadership

My Facebook page and group is ClaimYourDestiny or you can follow me on Twitter @JulieHogbin. Visit ClaimYourDestiny.global for more articles and up to date information, plus various other social media channels and Linkedin. My hashtag is #ConsciousLeadership if you would like to find me.

There are seven days in the week and someday isn't one of them!

ClaimYourDestiny.global
@JulieHogbin
#ConsciousLeadership

Motives and motivation are a matter of choice — yours! Choose well, look at why you believe what you believe, and question it. Listen to the answers of the questions you ask and you will create a different future if you really want to.

My final questions to you are:

- How much do you want to change?

- How willing are you to do what is required?

- What do you need to do right now?

Good luck with whatever it is you want to do. Here's to your fabulous success; you know where to find me.

Julie xx

www.ingramcontent.com/pod-product-compliance
Lightning Source LLC
Chambersburg PA
CBHW070334220526
45467CB00001B/131